Themes, Prayers, and Intercessions

Cycle B of the Lectionary

by

Rev. Nathan Mitchell, O.S.B.

WORLD LIBRARY PUBLICATIONS, INC.

5040 N. Ravenswood, Chicago, Illinois 60640

NIHIL OBSTAT: Rev. Lawrence J. Mick, Censor Deputatus
IMPRIMATUR: Rev. Msgr. August J. Kramer, Administrator, Sede Vacante,
Archdiocese of Cincinnati, November 15, 1972

CONTENTS

Introduction

The present volume for Cycle B is similar in purpose and format to the two earlier volumes of *Themes, Prayers, and Intercessions* published for Cycles A and C of the revised Lectionary for Sundays and major feasts. The suggested themes, homily notes and some of the invitations to the General Intercessions were provided by *The Grail* of England, whereas I have contributed the remaining elements.

The scope of a book like this is quite modest. First, it is not a "liturgical book" in the sense that a sacramentary, lectionary or missal is. The purpose of *Themes, Prayers, and Intercessions* is not to provide more liturgical texts, but rather suggestions for celebrants and liturgy teams responsible for planning Eucharistic celebrations. What Fr. Richard Ling remarked in his introduction to Cycle A of this series should be reiterated: ". . . compositions like *Themes, Prayers, and Intercessions* have a rightful place in the hands of those who plan liturgies only if they are not misused. Misuse means picking them up at the last minute and following them 'body and bones.' " It should be clear that a literal, unimaginative adherence to the suggestions in a book like this one will only perpetuate liturgies that are dull, vacuous and, in a word, deadly. And God knows the People of God have a right to expect better service than that!

Secondly, the question of liturgical "themes" deserves a comment. Themes imposed on the liturgy from without are of questionable value. They frequently exhibit a twisting of the biblical and liturgical texts to suit particular whims. On the other hand, themes derived from the biblical readings, themes selected in order to underscore the basic sense and direction of the liturgical texts, can be of immense service in planning the music, the homily, and the occasional comments for a service. The themes in this book were selected with those factors in mind.

In this connection, permit me a digression about the use of commentary in the liturgy. The General Instruction which accompanied the publication of the *Roman Missal* of Paul VI outlined several instances where comments could be introduced: the beginning of the celebration (to establish the general theme of a day or season); before the readings (a short summary of the contents, or an explanatory word which sets the selection in appropriate context); before the Eucharistic prayer; and before the final dismissal.

The point to be made here is this: it is not necessary, and probably not desirable, to introduce comments at every point where they

5

are permitted. Indeed, one of the major problems in the present liturgical reform is that it has been, up to now, almost exclusively verbal. Powerful communicative non-verbal elements (such as gesture, dance, instrumental music, silence) have not been fully explored. One of our colossal problems is a liturgy that threatens to "talk itself to death."

It is, therefore, imperative that attention be paid to the specific nature of liturgical discourse; and that discourse is, in my opinion, "mythic." By "mythic" I mean neither fable, nor falsehood, nor factual history. Rather, "mythic" discourse is the sort of language employed when men confront realities they cannot fully grasp or penetrate by rational reflection. All language about death, for instance, is mythic. It represents the human attempt to grapple with an experience that is not fully understandable. (Obviously people who have died usually don't return to talk about it — and, even if they did, it is doubtful that we would understand them!) The bane of the sequential Western mind is that it wishes to classify everything as logical or illogical, rational or irrational. But the liturgy speaks a mythic language, a language that is pre-rational, pre-discursive or, if you like, "metalogical."

The mythic language of the liturgy is the vehicle by which the Christian community comes to grips with the most fundamental meaning and purpose of its life: the dying and rising of Jesus, and our common death and rebirth in him. The worship which expresses and celebrates this fact can never be fully rational, fully logical or fully intelligible. Its language will inevitably remain somewhat quirky, a little odd, a little out of the ordinary. It presupposes a community of converted initiates; it presupposes an experience of God which breaks the bonds of conventional language; it presupposes that ambiguous condition of Christian man, the justified sinner.

This digression about liturgical language has been made to provide some background for my contention that one should be extremely judicious about the comments he chooses to add to the liturgical texts. The ideas contained in *Themes, Prayers, and Intercessions* are there to help in this process of careful selection: **BUT THEY REMAIN ONLY SUGGESTIONS.** In a given celebration one might elect to adopt only one or two ideas; or he might choose to comment only at the introduction to the liturgy; or he might want to make use only of the ideas for general intercessions. It goes without saying that such selection has to be made with the music and homily well in mind. If this is done, a liturgy can be planned that is integral in design, faithful to the biblical texts, and creatively pastoral.

Finally, allow me a word about the relation between *Themes, Prayers, and Intercessions* and the texts officially approved for use in the liturgy. The suggestions in this volume are not intended as replacements, but as examples of the way official texts can be pastorally adapted or, when desirable, expanded. Thus, for example, the English translation of the prayers in the *Roman Missal* of Paul VI, due to be ready for use by the first Sunday of Advent, 1972, will contain *ad libitum* introductions for prayers like the collect and the postcommunion. This present volume contains similar introductions for the purpose, again, of illustrating possible adaptations of texts in the missal or the sacramentary.

In conclusion, I should like to express my thanks to World Library Publications, Inc., especially to Mr. Omer Westendorf, Miss Betty Zins, Miss Diane Schaik, Fr. Paschal Varnskuhler, O.F.M., and Mr. Tyrrell Keller for their kind interest and support in this project. I should also like to thank my abbot, the Right Reverend Gabriel Verkamp, O.S.B., and the community of my brothers at St. Meinrad Archabbey for the opportunity to do this work in an atmosphere of peace and fraternal charity.

FR. NATHAN MITCHELL, O.S.B.
St. Meinrad Archabbey
St. Meinrad, Indiana

First Sunday of Advent

INTRODUCTION:

A culture which relies on instantaneous results finds waiting tedious and unprofitable. It is sobering to realize that God has been waiting for us longer than we have been waiting for him. He waits for us to give up our petty attempts to wring the most out of life, so that he can give us life itself: Jesus Christ.

INVITATION TO PENITENTIAL RITE:

Brothers and sisters, let us prepare for Christ's coming in glory by seeking his healing presence even in those drab moments of failure when he seems painfully absent.

FORM C: *(Optional invocations)*

You will come as a Light to shine in our darkness: Lord, have mercy.
You will come as a Shepherd to console and comfort: Christ . . .
You will come as a Brother to heal our sinfulness: Lord . . .

OPENING PRAYER:

Let us pray that the coming of Christ will heal broken lives, comfort the hopeless, and bring all men a refreshing change of heart and mind.

READINGS:

1) **Is. 63:16-17,19; 64:1,3-8.** We wait for God to come and save us, but he also waits for our return to him. Our God is not a bored and distant monarch, but a watchful Father.

2) **1 Cor. 1:3-9.** While we wait for Christ's appearing, the faithful Spirit brings us gifts of strength and peace.

3) **Mk. 13:33-37.** The man who sleeps away his life will miss its most significant moment. Stay awake, then, and be alert for Christ's coming.

HOMILY NOTES:

● However happy and successful life may be, it is incomplete without God. In times of trouble and distress we know how much we need him. Meanwhile we wait until all things are brought together under Christ, when he will come to take all creation to his Father.

- As we wait we have the Spirit in us, filling us with his gifts and the love of Christ, helping us to spread the Good News of his coming and to bring men the same hope that we have. We do not know when Christ will come — we must stay awake, awake to the signs of the Kingdom around us, awake to the opportunities of serving others, whether in our own families, in our parish, or in the wider community beyond the frontiers of the Church.

- We must also stir ourselves up to impatience for Christ's coming. The sooner his Kingdom on earth is achieved, the sooner he will come. "Come, Lord Jesus."

GENERAL INTERCESSIONS:

Invitation: The first reading of today's Mass reminds us that God is a Father, a Redeemer. Let us approach this Father with the loving confidence of children, as we pray: **LORD, COME TO OUR HELP.**

1. That a world grown old with wars and division may become new with Christ's own life, we pray to the Lord.

2. That men who wait without hope may find a new source of confidence in Christ's promise to come again, we . . .

3. That those who suffer blindness of heart may experience the light of Christ shining through the darkness, we . . .

4. That men addicted to violence and power may turn their hearts to the Christ who came as a servant, we . . .

5. That peace may visit the hearts and homes of all families this Advent season, we . . .

*(Additional invocations)*_____

Conclusion: Father, we wait for the coming of Christ your Son, confident that you will never disappoint us. As we wait, help us become what you have called us to be: a priestly people that offers you praise and prayer, through Christ our Lord.

ADDITIONAL INVITATION TO COMMUNION:

Behold the Master who bids us stay awake and prepare for his coming! This is the Lamb of God, etc.

PRAYER AFTER COMMUNION:

Today's Gospel contains the admonition of Christ: "Stay awake, because you do not know when the master of the house is coming." Strengthened by the bread of life, let us pray that we may be alert to the ways Christ comes to us daily — at home, at work, at recreation.

Second Sunday of Advent

THEME: THE DESERT

INTRODUCTION:

The desert is an ambiguous place. It can strengthen or demoralize; it can cause a man to drink in hope or wither into despair; it can renew a life or destroy it. Crossing the desert means coming to terms with ourselves, converting our hearts to prepare the way for Christ's coming.

INVITATION TO PENITENTIAL RITE:

John the Baptist cried out in the desert for true conversion and repentance. As we prepare for this Eucharist, let us honestly admit our failings and renew our baptismal promise of fidelity to Christ.

FORM C: *(Optional invocations)*

You alone can help us love light more than darkness: Lord, have mercy.

You alone have made atonement for our sins: Christ . . .
You alone can fill our emptiness and need: Lord . . .

OPENING PRAYER:

Let us pray for the readiness to welcome Christ wherever, whenever, and in whomever he may reveal himself.

READINGS:

1) **Is. 40:1-5,9-11.** God's mercy is mightily creative; it makes deserts become highways, and mountains become plains. It casts out fear once and for all.

2) **2 Pt. 3:8-14.** Christians hope not merely for improved conditions of life, but for life in a creation that is completely new.

3) **Mk. 1:1-8.** John the Baptist preaches repentance and promises a new baptism with water and the Holy Spirit.

HOMILY NOTES:

● In the desert the Israelites first heard the call to be God's people and were prepared for their role. In the desert John the Baptist proclaimed his message of the coming of Christ. It is to the desert that we must go to hear the message.

• The desert has no amenities; there is only God and, too, a total need of God. In the desert we realize our emptiness before God. The desert is a crisis place, where decisions are a matter of life and death, God or self. There is no room for compromise, no margin of error, no possibility of procrastination.

• Times of stress, worry, and bereavement are "desert" experiences; but we must also look for other opportunities to simplify our lives, clear out some of the clutter and come to terms with essentials. It is vital for us to hear John's message of joy, and to prepare for the newness of life coming for those who will meet Christ, those who have made the "rough ways plain."

GENERAL INTERCESSIONS:

Invitation: The call to holiness is a universal vocation in the Church. Let us pray that we do not allow a thirst for ease and comfort to replace our desire for justice and holiness among men. Our response is: **COME TO SAVE US, LORD.**

1. That men whose lives have been withered by our lack of concern may be aided by our conversion of heart, we pray to the Lord.

2. That all who live in deserts of poverty and despair may be encouraged by our concrete efforts to assist them, we . . .

3. That young and old alike may be granted a deeper insight into the working of God's Spirit in their lives, we . . .

4. That men may direct their talents and energies to the cause of peace and not to the continuance of hostile divisions, we . . .

*(Additional invocations)*_____

Conclusion: Speak to us, Father, as you spoke, of old, to Israel in the desert. Help us overcome our fears, our cowardice, our fond illusions, and give us true repentance by sending your Spirit of consolation, through Christ our Lord.

ADDITIONAL INVITATION TO COMMUNION:
Behold the One who is coming to forgive and console!

PRAYER AFTER COMMUNION:
"What we are waiting for is what he promised: the new heavens and new earth." Let us pray that this communion may increase our thirst for justice and strengthen our hands to work for peace.

11

Third Sunday of Advent

INTRODUCTION:

Nothing is as welcome as good news. And the good news today is help for the poor, comfort for broken hearts, liberty for physical and moral prisoners. These things are not mere pious promises; they are the task and goals of every Christian. Christ's coming will fulfill these goals, and we await him by listening to his Word and celebrating the freedom meal of the Eucharist.

INVITATION TO PENITENTIAL RITE:

As we prepare to celebrate the mystery of salvation, let us recall the times we have rejected Christ's coming through our hardness and insensitivity toward others.

FORM C: *(Optional invocations)*

You were anointed to bring good news to the poor: Lord, have mercy.

You came to bring men freedom and integrity: Christ . . .

You will never disappoint those who trust you: Lord . . .

OPENING PRAYER:

Let us pray that our own lives may bring wisdom, light and truth to a world aching for justice and authenticity.

READINGS:

1) **Is. 61:1-2,10-11.** To men who are captives of hopeless futility, Isaiah rings out a comforting message of hope.

2) **I Thes. 5:16-24.** Writing to the Thessalonians, Paul counsels happiness, prayer and thanksgiving to all who wait for Christ's coming.

3) **Jn. 1:6-8,19-28.** John the Baptist provides the classic example of witnessing: he points not to himself, but to the Light coming into the world.

HOMILY NOTES:

● We can think of "Advent" in three tenses: he came, he comes, he will come. Isaiah describes the effect of Christ's coming: men renewed as the earth is renewed by spring. Historically, he really came and brought our renewal. He is here today, among us as we gather in his name, listen to his word, and celebrate the Eucharist.

12

- We prepare ourselves for this daily coming to us, and for his coming in glory. We prepare ourselves by a new start as John the Baptist's converts did; a real conversion, a starting afresh, a radical rethinking of our lives and our attitudes toward one another.

- We remove the mountains of our selfishness, fill in the valleys of our lack of care and indifference, so that the way is smooth with nothing between us and Christ as he comes to us.

GENERAL INTERCESSIONS:

Invitation: John the Baptist knew when to speak and when to keep silent, when to assert himself and when to step into the background. Let us ask God to free us of that exaggerated self-importance which sometimes stands in the way of Christ's coming. Our response is: **COME, LORD, LIGHT OF THE WORLD.**

1. That as Church we may witness to the truth through humble and honest lives, we pray to the Lord.

2. That we might exclude from our hearts whatever is vicious and dehumanizing, we . . .

3. That the poor, the blind, and the captive may receive the light of Jesus' Good News, we . . .

4. For all who are ill with incurable diseases, and for those who minister to their medical and pastoral needs, we . . .

5. That the anticipation of Christmas joy may unite families in the desire to work for the alleviation of human misery, we . . .

*(Additional invocations)*_____

Conclusion: Father of the poor, we ask you to let your mercy shine on all who suffer. Let us see your face in the happiness of children and the serenity of the aged, so that we may rejoice in your love every day of our lives, through Christ our Lord.

ADDITIONAL INVITATION TO COMMUNION:
Behold the Light of the World!

PRAYER AFTER COMMUNION:
"John came as a witness, as a witness to speak for the Light." Let us pray that the bread of mercy which we have shared may become, through us, a light which conquers darkness and raises up the lowly.

13

Fourth Sunday of Advent

THEME: DAVID'S PROMISED DESCENDANT

INTRODUCTION:

Too often we think of mystery as a clever riddle aimed only at skillful thinkers or police detectives. But in the Bible, "mystery" is God's plan for salvation which grows quietly throughout history and gives real meaning to every human event. Today God's mystery emerges as a proclamation of Jesus Christ, David's descendant, who gives final significance to all human life.

INVITATION TO PENITENTIAL RITE:

My friends in the Lord, God's Word urges us strongly to renew our decision to live a life patterned on that of Jesus. Let us pause to ask pardon for those times when we have been indecisive and half-hearted in our commitment to the Lord.

FORM C: *(Optional invocations)*

You are the Morning Star bringing light to the world: Lord, have mercy.
You are the Son of David, the fulfillment of God's promise: Christ . . .
You are the Son of Mary, and brother to every man: Lord . . .

OPENING PRAYER:

Let us pray, together with Mary the Mother of Jesus, that we may ponder in our hearts the great mystery of God's love revealed in Christ.

READINGS:

1) **2 Sm. 7:1-5,8-11,16.** David had plans to build God a house — but the Lord had other ideas. Rather, God would live among men and build a house for David.

2) **Rom. 16:25-27.** Paul writes that God's hidden mystery has been revealed in a person: Jesus Christ, the Wisdom and Glory of the Father.

3) **Lk. 1:26-38.** Luke draws upon the Old Testament theme of the virgin daughter of Zion, as he presents the story of a woman whose Son would fulfill God's promise to David.

HOMILY NOTES:

● David wanted to build a temple for God. God said that this was not what he wanted. He wanted to found for David a lasting royal house from which the Savior would come. David agrees.

- Mary wanted to live a quiet married life with her husband Joseph. God said he wanted her, by the power of the Holy Spirit, to have a son who would be called the "Son of God." Mary agrees: "Let what you have said be done to me."

- Jesus Christ is the Good News for us. In our following of him we too must be prepared to agree to what he wants for us, even if it means scrapping our own well-laid plans. This is not easy. But Paul tells us that Christ is the one able to give us the strength to live the way he did.

GENERAL INTERCESSIONS:

Invitation: Through baptism into Christ we became the descendants of the Father, and our life is now a journey back to his house. We need the strength of prayer to make that journey; so let us offer our petitions, as we respond: **LORD, SHOW US THE WAY.**

1. That our preparations for the coming feast of Christmas may inspire us to share the good things of earth with the needy, we pray to the Lord.

2. That parents may show their children the beauty of a life based on prayer and fidelity to the Gospel, we . . .

3. For all children, especially those who are unwanted and neglected, we . . .

4. For those who have not yet heard the Good News of Christ, and for those who go forth to preach it, we . . .

5. That men bent on destruction and war may be converted to the way of peace, we . . .

(Additional invocations) _____

Conclusion: Father of mercy, you sent your Son as a Way that leads to holiness, a Truth that conquers falsehood, and a Life that destroys death. Help us follow the way Jesus walked, and bring us back home to you. We make our prayer through Christ our Lord.

ADDITIONAL INVITATION TO COMMUNION:
Behold the Wisdom and Glory of the Father!

PRAYER AFTER COMMUNION:
"He alone is wisdom; give glory, therefore, to him through Jesus Christ forever and ever." Let us pray for the wisdom that comes from responsive listening to God's Word in creation, in scripture, and in the lives of one another.

Christmas Midnight

THEME: PEACE AND JOY

INTRODUCTION:

Night is the setting for two great Christian festivals: the birth of Jesus and his rising from death into glory. In many respects both feasts affirm the same thing: there is no darkness so powerful that it can destroy Christ's light, no sin so destructive that it cannot be overcome through the presence of Emmanuel, God-with-us. This is the night which brings peace to the restless and joy to the frightened.

INVITATION TO PENITENTIAL RITE:

Beloved in Christ, the child born to us this night came to save us from our sins. Let us resolve, at this Mass, to put aside once for all any attachment to self-centeredness.

FORM C: *(Optional invocations)*

Your coming brings peace to the weary: Lord, have mercy.
Your presence puts an end to sin: Christ . . .
Your love reveals the Father's tender care: Lord . . .

OPENING PRAYER:

Let us joyfully pray that Christ's birth may unite all men in the one Spirit of peace and of hope.

READINGS:

1) **Is. 9:1-6.** When God appears, darkness vanishes. Isaiah proclaims that a great light has shone, that no one needs to be afraid anymore.

2) **Ti. 2:11-14.** God's name is compassion and mercy; his love is not restricted to men of rank and privilege, but is all-embracing. As Paul writes, salvation is now possible "for the whole human race."

3) **Lk. 2:1-14.** The Savior, born of Mary, is Christ the Lord, the Father's everlasting glory.

HOMILY NOTES:

● Modern man is searching for basically very simple things. He wants happiness and joy, and the peace on which joy is founded. Isaiah, surely looking into the future, said that these would come with the coming of the Messiah: "You have made their gladness greater, you have made their joy increase." "For to us a child is born, to us a Son is given."

● The shepherds were given "news of great joy, a joy to be shared by the whole people," and were directed to go and look for a new born baby, a child who is "Christ the Lord," the Messiah or Savior — God. He is the Prince of Peace.

● Real joy and peace are to be found in one person only, in Christ. Let us resolve to keep Christ at the center of our lives; then we will experience the joy and peace that only he can give.

GENERAL INTERCESSIONS:

Invitation: When Jesus was born there were no fanfares, no parades. Born poor, he lived and died the same way. Let us open our hearts to this child of poverty as we pray: **LORD, DWELL AMONG US.**

1. That men who govern and guide the affairs of nations may follow Christ's way of peace, we pray to the Lord.

2. That during this Christmas season the poor and the outcast may find a welcome among us, we . . .

3. That men might direct their energies away from exploitation and towards feeding the hungry and clothing the naked, we . . .

4. That the joy of this day may become a way of life and not merely a momentary sentiment, we . . .

5. That men who are frightened and discouraged may receive hope from Emmanuel, God-with-us, we pray . . .

*(Additional invocations)*_____

Conclusion: We give you thanks, Father, for speaking your Word in promise and for sending that same Word to share, fully and personally, in our human condition. Help us to reflect the peace and joy of this night every moment of our lives, for we make this prayer through Christ our Lord.

ADDITIONAL INVITATION TO COMMUNION:

Behold the One whose birth brought us the light of salvation!

PRAYER AFTER COMMUNION:

"You have made their joy increase; they rejoice in your presence." Let us pray that our communion in Christ's body and blood may bring us that kind of joy which is deep and abiding, precisely because it is shared with all men.

Christmas Dawn

THEME: LOVE SAVES US

INTRODUCTION:

Our God seeks men, seeks them vigorously. He reveals himself to people who are lowly and unimpressive — like the shepherds of this morning's Gospel. God is not impressed by elegance and class, but by simple, joyful hearts. To such as these the Father's saving love is manifested in all its human-ness.

INVITATION TO PENITENTIAL RITE:

Brothers and sisters, God's love sought and saved us even while we were still sinners. Let us ask pardon for the times we have forfeited that love by our own lack of charity.

FORM C: *(Optional invocations)*

Jesus, Bright Star of Morning: Lord, have mercy.
Jesus, Savior of all the earth: Christ . . .
Jesus, living kindness and love of the Father: Lord . . .

OPENING PRAYER:

Let us pray that this celebration of Christmas may bring a new dawn of peace and freedom to mankind.

READINGS:

1) **Is. 62:11-12.** God's coming creates a holy and redeemed people.

2) **Ti. 3:4-7.** The birth of Jesus manifests God's compassion and re-creates a people through water and the Holy Spirit.

3) **Lk. 2:15-20.** The shepherds praised God when they saw Mary, Joseph, and the child.

HOMILY NOTES:

● St. Paul tells us plainly that we have not done anything to deserve salvation; we are saved simply because of God's love and compassion for us. God loves us, so God saves us. It is as simple and wonderful as that.

- We have not earned or paid for a Savior. It is wholly God's work. The only trouble is that normally we don't see much value in things we get for nothing. We like to feel we have earned things, paid for them by human effort. We have difficulty accepting "free" salvation.

- We must accept it, but we need humility to do so. Some people despair of ever being worthy of God. A person will say, "I am not good enough." But the whole point of Christ's teaching is that it is God who saves us. We must keep our eyes on God, not on ourselves.

GENERAL INTERCESSIONS:

Invitation: Jesus' birth reveals God's kindness and gives us rebirth through the Holy Spirit. Let us give him thanks and rededicate ourselves to the task of sharing such love with one another, as we pray: **LORD, RENEW US BY YOUR LOVE.**

1. That the Church may always be responsive to God's initiative in sending salvation to the world, we pray to the Lord.

2. That sinners find, in this feast of Christmas, a new confidence in God's tender compassion, we . . .

3. That we may look for Christ's presence especially among the forgotten and the lonely, we . . .

4. That men in positions of power may use their influence to promote truth and justice in the world, we . . .

5. That Christians everywhere may share more creatively in the work of spreading Christ's Gospel of peace, we . . .

*(Additional invocations)*_____

Conclusion: Father, your kindness and love have appeared to us in the gift of Jesus your Son. Help us to realize that the work of salvation begins and ends in you, that we are the servants of the Gospel, and not its masters. We make our prayer through Christ our Lord.

ADDITIONAL INVITATION TO COMMUNION:
Behold the kindness and love of God our Savior!

PRAYER AFTER COMMUNION:
"He saved us by means of the cleansing water of rebirth and by renewing us with the Holy Spirit." Let us pray that the food we have received at this table may make us living signs of God's covenant, sealed in our flesh through Jesus and the Spirit.

19

Christmas Day

THEME: GOD MADE VISIBLE

INTRODUCTION:

God is not some misty, behind-the-scenes potentate. He involved himself so concretely with his creation that he has become visible in a man, Jesus our Mediator. Of this same Jesus we are members through Baptism, and it is our task to make the Father visible to men of our day.

INVITATION TO PENITENTIAL RITE:

My friends, Jesus' coming was intended to bring us a fuller, more abundant life. Let us reflect for a moment on those occasions when we have prevented the growth of his life in us through our being lukewarm.

FORM C: *(Optional invocations)*

Word of God, source of creation: Lord, have mercy.
Light and life of men: Christ . . .
Son of God, full of grace and truth. Lord . . .

OPENING PRAYER:

Let us pray that, as we listen to God speaking through the prophets and through Jesus, we may hear him speaking a message of love in today's world also.

READINGS:

1) **Is. 52:7-10.** Isaiah calls "beautiful" those people who bring news of peace and happiness. Happy, indeed, are such persons, for they will see God face to face.

2) **Heb. 1:1-6.** God's last word to man is also his first. The Word through whom all things were made is the Word we hear in Jesus.

3) **Jn. 1:1-18.** In our Gospel selection from John we listen to a hymn about the Word and Son who is nearest the Father's heart.

HOMILY NOTES:

● People sometimes ask "What is God like?" In fact, we know what God is like. For years people had only a hazy idea of God. He spoke to them, but only through other men. Then he did more than men ever dreamt possible: God sent his own Son to us.

• God the Son, who had forever been with the Father, became a man: "The Word was made flesh," a real man of flesh and blood and human spirit. He entered fully into the human condition: "He lived among us." In him we see what God is like: "We saw his glory, the glory that is his as the only Son of the Father, full of grace (i.e., love) and truth."

• If we would know God, we need only look at Jesus, who is God's Son. He will lead us to the Father: "It is only the Son, who is nearest to the Father's heart, who has made him known."

GENERAL INTERCESSIONS:

Invitation: Jesus is the sacrament of God's love for the world; and we, as Church, are the sacrament of unity among men. Conscious of our mission to be a leaven of unity in the world, let us offer prayer to the Father. Our response is: **LORD, MAKE US ONE IN YOU.**

1. That all preachers of God's Word may be given courage and enthusiasm in announcing the Good News of salvation, we pray to the Lord.

2. That all men may discover a common bond of brotherhood in Christ the Savior, we . . .

3. That the Gospel values of peace and justice may permeate the structures of human governments, we . . .

4. That all men may learn that God's truth in Christ is stronger than brute force or human reasoning, we . . .

5. That our celebration of Christmas may mark the beginning of a renewed desire for unity among men of different races, colors, and religions, we . . .

*(Additional invocations)*_____

Conclusion: We thank you, Father, that you have not hidden your love, but have made it visible and available to us in Jesus, your Word made flesh. Keep us faithful to our vocation as a sacrament of unity in the world, so that all men may come to know you and the Son you sent. We make our prayer through Christ our Lord.

ADDITIONAL INVITATION TO COMMUNION:
Behold God's love made visible to us!

PRAYER AFTER COMMUNION:
"He is the radiant light of God's glory." Let us pray that this sacrament which has made us one body, one spirit in Christ, may bring unity and peace to all mankind.

Holy Family
Sunday in Octave of Christmas

THEME: FAMILY LIFE

INTRODUCTION:

The Holy Family offers us a model of unity within diversity. Jesus, Mary, and Joseph each had unique and diverse vocations in God's plan, yet they were united in a community of love and mutual support. Christian family life, based on this model, will respect individuality without giving up the values of common sharing.

INVITATION TO PENITENTIAL RITE:

Brothers and sisters, no family can grow in Christ, except on the basis of mutual respect and forgiveness. Let us ask pardon for those times we have refused to forgive one another.

FORM C: *(Optional invocations)*

You were a child of poverty and a friend of those in need: Lord, have mercy.

You help us grow, as you grew, in wisdom and maturity: Christ . . .

You unite all men into the one family of God's children: Lord . . .

OPENING PRAYER:

Let us pray for strength to live up to the responsibilities of membership in our own families and in the larger families of Church and world.

READINGS:

1) **Sir. 3:2-6, 12-14.** The author of Sirach reminds us that kindness to parents will result in atonement for our sins and failings.

2) **Col. 3:12-21.** Paul writes that what makes families Christian is the love which forgives all things, hopes for all things, endures all things.

3) **Lk. 2:22-40.** In his Gospel Luke gives us a picture of the Holy Family in the Temple. Inspired by the Spirit, Simeon prophesies about Jesus' destiny as a sign of contradiction.

HOMILY NOTES:

● Each day we tell our Father in heaven that we want his Kingdom to come on earth. We cannot change many things in the world, but our influence does extend over our own homes and our own families.

● In the family we learn to love, to have tolerance for one another. Through the family we learn to relate to the wider community in Christian love. Husbands and wives giving their whole love and service to each other are doing what God wants of them.

● This, for married people, is their way to God, and this is how their children learn to love God, too. Children develop in their relationship to their parents, passing from implicit obedience to respectful attention and, through loving friendship, to the constant care which old age calls for.

GENERAL INTERCESSIONS:

Invitation: Family love is never without its moments of pain and frustration. We ask God for patience and faithful dedication to one another, as we pray: **LORD, HELP US GROW IN LOVE.**

1. That members of families may understand their roles as servants of one another, we pray to the Lord.

2. That both old and young may find in Christ a basis for mutual respect and understanding, we . . .

3. That all men may realize their vocation to form a single family united in a common search for justice and peace, we . . .

4. That Christians may overcome their divisions and discover once again their unity through one faith, one Lord, and one baptism, we . . .

5. That families broken by war, imprisonment, and exile may be united once more, we . . .

*(Additional invocations)*_____

Conclusion: Father, you are the source and foundation of all family life. Strengthen us to overcome the irritations and disappointments of our lives together, and help us each day to begin anew our search for unity in love. We ask this through Christ our Lord.

ADDITIONAL INVITATION TO COMMUNION:

Behold Christ the Lord, the promised salvation of God!

PRAYER AFTER COMMUNION:

"The child grew to maturity, and he was filled with wisdom; and God's favor was with him." Let us pray that the one bread we have received may bring us closer together as family, as Church, and as citizens of a world that seeks a deeper meaning in life.

January 1: Solemnity of Mary, Mother of God*

THEME: RESPONSE

INTRODUCTION:

Great people are not necessarily the ones who talk a lot or even do a lot. To be great means to be responsive, simply and quietly, to God's action in the concrete circumstances of life. Such was Mary's greatness: she was so alive to God's Word that this same Word took up life in her.

INVITATION TO PENITENTIAL RITE:

Quiet, responsive listening is difficult for us who live in a culture that is bombarded by noise. Let us reflect on those times when we have failed to listen to others and ignored their cry for help.

FORM C: *(Optional invocations)*

You listened to our cry for help and came to save us: Lord, have mercy.

Your Spirit cries out in us, "Abba, Father": Christ . . .

You made us sons and heirs of your Kingdom: Lord . . .

OPENING PRAYER:

Let us pray for the ability to hear God's Word both in the midst of hectic activity and in moments of quiet reflection.

READINGS:

1) **Nm. 6:22-27.** In the Old Testament God's presence was associated with his Name, invoked in blessing. Conscious that Christ, God's Name made visible, will bless us always with his presence, we listen to this reading from Numbers.

2) **Gal. 4:4-7.** Paul writes that Christ was born subject to the Law in order to free us for sonship in the Spirit.

3) **Lk. 2:16-21.** Luke tells us that Mary treasured the memory of all that happened when Jesus was born.

HOMILY NOTES:

● Mary was wonderfully blessed in the child she bore. The words spoken to her in Nazareth are almost an echo of the blessing given to Aaron, which occur in the first reading. "May the Lord let his face shine on you and be gracious to you."

---

*The Mass for World Day of Peace may be celebrated on January 1 or on another day, with permission of the local Ordinary. For alternate Mass, see p. 152.

- Mary's Son was the fulfillment of all the hopes of the Jewish nation. Through her, God shows that his own chosen people have now become ready to have the Messiah in their midst. Too often in their history, Christians have overlooked or hidden the truth that Jesus and Mary were Jews.

- Mary, though she willingly accepted the role as Mother of the Messiah, did not realize its immensity nor the direction in which it would lead her. She therefore "pondered these things in her heart," not merely on that one occasion in the Temple but to the end of her life.

- Mary is one of the links between the Church of the Old Covenant and the Church of the New. She is the sign of fulfillment, liberation, and love. Because of her consenting to be Mother of God we can receive the Spirit of her Son into our hearts.

GENERAL INTERCESSIONS:

Invitation: We can respond to God's invitation to become his sons and daughters only because he has first responded to our deepest needs and desires. Full of confidence in his providential care, let us pray: **LORD, FILL US WITH YOUR LIFE.**

1. That men may come to learn that responsive listening is more important than frantic activity, we pray to the Lord.

2. For those in the Church who are committed to a life of contemplative reflection on God's Word, we pray . . .

3. That the Church may witness to those deeply feminine values revealed in the life of Mary, we . . .

4. That pastors and parishioners may share their insights into God's action in the world through increased dialogue and prayer, we . . .

*(Additional invocations)*_____

Conclusion: Father, our hearts are often choked by anxieties about our families, our jobs, our attempts to get ahead in life. Give us the wisdom to listen quietly and confidently for your voice, even when turmoil and frustration threaten to overwhelm us. We make our prayer through Christ our Lord.

ADDITIONAL INVITATION TO COMMUNION:

Behold Jesus, Son of Mary and brother of all men!

PRAYER AFTER COMMUNION:

"The proof that you are sons is that God has sent the Spirit of his Son into our hearts." Let us pray that all of us who have eaten at the Lord's table may be filled with the same Spirit of sonship and holiness.

Second Sunday After Christmas

THEME: GOD'S WORD

INTRODUCTION:

The celebration of Christmas means more than rejoicing over a past event. Christ has indeed come in our flesh — yet we confess that he is still to come. That is because the mystery of the Incarnation will not be complete until the entire creation is fully summed up in Christ as Lord. The Incarnation is a beginning that thrusts us forward and inspires us to work for the full coming of God's Kingdom.

INVITATION TO PENITENTIAL RITE:

Brothers and sisters, we often allow ourselves to be so concerned about the past that we do not hear God calling us forward to greater maturity in Christ. Let us ask pardon for the times we have resisted God's call to greater growth.

FORM C: *(Optional invocations)*

You live and grow among us through Word and Sacrament: Lord, have mercy.

You lead us from past failure to selfless love: Christ . . .

You call us to be holy and spotless in your presence: Lord . . .

OPENING PRAYER:

Let us pray that God may open our eyes to all that is true and beautiful in the world he created by his Word.

READINGS:

1) **Sir. 24:1-4, 8-12.** In the literature of the Old Testament, Wisdom was not an abstract idea; it was an expression of God's presence and his creative dynamism. The reading from Sirach describes how Wisdom pitched its tent among men.

2) **Eph. 1:3-6, 15-18.** Like Sirach, Paul also speaks of Wisdom — the Wisdom which took human form in the person of Jesus Christ.

3) **Jn. 1:1-18.** John praises Christ the Word, the Wisdom which leads men to know the truth about God.

HOMILY NOTES:

● In the Bible, God's Word has power. When God speaks, something happens. "God said, 'Let there be light' and there was light."

- God's Word is the expression of what and who he is. The writer of our first reading thought God's Wisdom so great as to be a person. He was foreshadowing St. John's writing in his Gospel about Jesus the Word: God's creating Word, God's teaching Word, God's saving Word.

- We cannot know the Father; so he sent his Son, his Word, to tell us about God and show us what God is like. By doing as Jesus did, living a life of care and concern for others, we come to know him and make him known.

GENERAL INTERCESSIONS:

Invitation: Paul declared in today's second reading that God chose us personally in Christ, before the world was made. Even if we are sometimes unsure about how interested we are in God, we can be quite confident that God is vitally interested in us. Let us, then, offer prayer joyfully, as we respond: **WORD OF GOD, GROW IN US.**

1. That those powers in the world which still resist the coming of God's Kingdom may be led to a knowledge of the truth, we pray to the Lord.

2. That the Church may boldly proclaim the Gospel without compromising its difficult challenges, we pray . . .

3. For all who use their creative imagination to promote a better future for man, we . . .

4. For those who devote their lives to helping human beings grow to fuller personal maturity, we . . .

5. For those whom we have caused to stumble by our lukewarm commitment to Christ, we pray . . .

*(Additional invocations)*_____

Conclusion: You sent your Word, Father, as the true light of the world. We ask that this light may shine in us, and lead all men to share the blessings of a fuller life in your Son. We make our prayer through Christ our Lord.

ADDITIONAL INVITATION TO COMMUNION:

Behold Christ, whose life is the light of men!

PRAYER AFTER COMMUNION:

"All that came to be had life in him, and that life was the light of men." Let us pray that our share in this Eucharistic meal may be the sign of that day when all men will sit together at table in Christ's Kingdom.

Epiphany

THEME: UNIVERSAL SALVATION

INTRODUCTION:

Most of us are a little cynical about advertisements which promise, "Free! No strings attached!" Everyone, we figure, has his angle. But God's offer of salvation in Christ allows no such cynicism; it is utterly free and available to all men with faith and good will. Such is the message of Epiphany, Christ's free revelation to all the world.

INVITATION TO PENITENTIAL RITE:

My brothers and sisters, let us begin this Eucharist by asking ourselves how often we have restricted our faith and our charity, refusing to share it with those who live and work with us.

FORM C: *(Optional invocations)*

Lord Jesus, Dawning Light of a new creation: Lord, have mercy.
Lord Jesus, Savior of the poor and helpless: Christ . . .
Lord Jesus, true Peace for all nations: Lord . . .

OPENING PRAYER:

Let us pray that all men may come to share in the inheritance of Jesus Christ, since all have received the same promise of salvation.

READINGS:

1) **Is. 60:1-6.** We listen to a passage from Isaiah which describes a time when all men will see God's glory and unite in singing his praises.

2) **Eph. 3:2-3, 5-6.** Paul writes that the mystery revealed in Christ means salvation for *all* men, not for just the few.

3) **Mt. 2:1-12.** Guided by a star, the Wise Men seek out Christ and offer him gifts.

HOMILY NOTES:

● The prophets had always announced that God's mercy was for all men even though he had chosen to reveal himself through one people. Christ reiterated that he had come for all nations and, especially in the parables, warned Israel that others would be invited to the Kingdom.

● Christ's family tree included the names of three foreign women, and in his infancy the non-Jewish nations worshipped him as well as his own people.

- Thinking ourselves to be the new Chosen People, we have been exclusive, have not recognized that others than ourselves can have a real faith in Christ. At the same time, we have ignored Christ's commandment to love and to show his love in our lives.

- God's offer is open to all men; so he speaks through all languages, in different cultures, and at different times. We must not seek to confine God to our way of thinking and our customs. Every good element in the cultures of the nations and races contributes to our understanding of God's goodness. The Kingdom of God includes everybody who seeks to follow Christ with all his heart.

GENERAL INTERCESSIONS:

Invitation: There are many persons who seek Christ, but cannot seem to find him. It is easy for us who enjoy the riches of Christian life to become smug and complacent, to ignore those who grope painfully for the truth about God. Today let us open our hearts to such people, as we pray: **LORD, REVEAL YOURSELF TO ALL MEN.**

1. That all who seek God in sincerity of heart may find him revealed in Christian lives, we pray to the Lord.

2. That the Church may faithfully accomplish its mission to be a sacrament of hope for the world, we . . .

3. That Christ's special love for the poor may be reflected in our own efforts to improve their situation, we . . .

4. That we may not restrict our faith and charity to a special few, but rather share it joyfully with every person we meet, we . . .

5. That all of us may become more responsive to the universal call to holiness in the Church, we . . .

*(Additional invocations)*_____

Conclusion: Father, your Son has told us that, in seeking, we shall find. Help us search for your presence everywhere: in the faces of children, in the anguish of the sick and suffering, in the love of brother for brother. We make our prayer through Christ our Lord.

ADDITIONAL INVITATION TO COMMUNION:
Behold the Lord who comes in dawning brightness!

PRAYER AFTER COMMUNION:
"Arise, shine out, for your light has come; the glory of the Lord is rising on you." Let us pray that we may leave this Mass filled with the light which can bring happiness to a world plunged in darkness.

Baptism of the Lord*

THEME: BAPTISM INTO CHRIST

INTRODUCTION:

Baptism was a critical moment in Jesus' life, because it marked the inauguration of his public ministry as servant, preacher, and healer. Our Baptism into Christ means sharing his mission as servant and his destiny as risen Son of God. This is why we gather today, as a baptized community, to share table-fellowship with Christ and with one another.

INVITATION TO PENITENTIAL RITE:

Baptism is like life itself; it either grows and matures, or it shrivels up and dies. Let us pause to ask ourselves whether our baptismal commitment is steadily growing more vital, or steadily diminishing in importance.

FORM C: (Optional invocations)

By Baptism you create us as a new and holy people: Lord, have mercy.

By the gift of the Spirit, you make us sons and brothers: Christ . . .

By your body and blood, you give us a pledge of future glory: Lord . . .

OPENING PRAYER:

Let us pray that our baptism will be a constant source of growth in self-forgetting service to others.

READINGS:

1) **Is. 42:1-4, 6-7.** Isaiah's image of God's servant profoundly influenced the Gospel accounts of Christ's Baptism. Jesus was understood as the true servant, the one in whom his Father delighted.

2) **Acts 10:34-38.** The servant theme is heard again in our second reading. Jesus is the servant whom God anointed with the Holy Spirit and with power.

3) **Mk. 1:7-11.** Jesus' mission and destiny as servant are confirmed by the Father's voice and the Spirit's presence.

HOMILY NOTES:

● John the Baptist, announcing the imminent coming of the Redeemer, called the people to be baptized, to be plunged into the water to rise to new life, ready for Christ. Jesus, at the start of his

---

*NOTE: For Sundays between the Baptism of the Lord and Ash Wednesday, see Sundays of the Year, p. 72.

ministry, chose to begin as other men. He identified himself with our helplessness, with us in need of redemption; he rose from the water to be filled with the Spirit, and to be greeted by the voice of God as "My beloved Son."

● The Greek word for "son" can also mean "servant"; so Jesus is the servant in our first reading. He will free us, captive in the loneliness of our human situation, and open our blind eyes. Because this could be brought about only through his death, Jesus called his passion his Baptism. We make Christ's death and resurrection our own when we are baptized, when we die with Christ, and rise with him. We are "Christ-ened," made into Christs.

● We have to ratify the Baptism we received as infants, identify ourselves every day with Christ in his life and love and his fight against sin, and rise to new life in the Spirit of Christ, growing daily more like him.

GENERAL INTERCESSIONS:

Invitation: As persons dead and risen with Christ, we have become a holy nation, a priestly people. Let us manifest our share in Christ's priesthood by offering prayer for the needs of all men. Our response is: **LORD, MAKE US NEW PEOPLE.**

1. That the Church may always seek to serve rather than be served, we pray to the Lord.

2. That all Christians, baptized into the same Christ, may one day be able to share in the same Eucharistic table, we . . .

3. For all in our community who will soon be baptized into Christ, we . . .

4. That parents may nourish the baptismal life of their children through prayer and through lives of service, we . . .

*(Additional invocations)*_____

Conclusion: Lord Jesus, your Baptism meant the beginning of a way which led to the cross, death, and resurrection. Keep us on the same way, even when the times are difficult and the rewards seem small. We ask this of you who live and reign with the Father and the Holy Spirit, now and forever.

ADDITIONAL INVITATION TO COMMUNION:
Behold the beloved servant of God!

PRAYER AFTER COMMUNION:
"You are my Son, the Beloved; my favor rests on you." Let us pray that our reception of Christ's body and blood may keep us faithful to the promises we made at Baptism.

Ash Wednesday

THEME: PRAYER, FASTING, AND ALMSGIVING

INTRODUCTION:

Christians do penance not because they enjoy morbid suffering, but because they realize the need for a more adult conversion to the ways of God. Lent is thus a time for ridding ourselves of deep-rooted illusions about our relationship with Christ. It is a time for re-evaluating our priorities, for planting new seeds of hope and love, for sharing Christ's passion so as to share his glory. Prayer, fasting and almsgiving will help us cooperate in this work of grace.

INVITATION TO PENITENTIAL RITE:

Dear friends, we cannot remain childish and indecisive about our faith. Let us pause to reflect on the most significant ways in which we need to mature as members of Christ's body.

FORM C: *(Optional invocations)*

You taught us to seek and find you in prayer: Lord, have mercy.

You shared with us the Bread of your life and your teaching: Christ . . .

You emptied yourself, becoming poor and weak for our sake: Lord . . .

OPENING PRAYER:

Let us pray that we may rededicate ourselves this Lent to the search for closer union with God and with neighbor.

READINGS:

1) **Jl. 2:12-18.** The prophet Joel tells us that what God wants is a change of heart, not torn garments and a gloomy face.

2) **2 Cor. 5:20 — 6:2.** Paul indicates that our chief task as Christians is to become reconciled to God and to one another in Christ.

3) **Mt. 6:1-6, 16-18.** Jesus preaches a repentance that gets at the heart of the matter and doesn't count on outward appearances.

HOMILY NOTES:

● Lent is a time for trying to see where we stand before God, of re-assessing our attitudes and conduct towards those around us.

- There should be no element of fear, of gloom or resignation to self-imposed mortification. If our efforts do not heighten our love and awareness of God and neighbor, they are in vain. If they are ostentatious and earn us commendation, they are not in the spirit of the Gospel.

- Our renewed fervor should serve to deepen our realization of Christ's saving acts and of God's goodness and holiness. We should take every opportunity to share with others the joy and solemnity of the season when we celebrate the mysteries of Christ's death and resurrection.

GENERAL INTERCESSIONS:

Invitation: The season of Lent calls us to an interior conversion of heart which will bear fruit in the way we relate to others. In prayer let us turn to our God, who is rich in kindness, with the words: **LORD, HAVE MERCY.**

1. That during this Lenten season Christians may gain a more mature understanding of their responsibilities toward God and man, we pray to the Lord.

2. That we may take more seriously our vocation as disciples of a crucified Savior, we . . .

3. That we may stop seeking the easiest ways to follow Christ, and boldly take up the cross that leads to glory, we . . .

4. That we may more generously share our goods with the poor through fasting and almsgiving, we . . .

5. That our families may draw closer to the mind and heart of God through a prayerful reading of the Scriptures, we . . .

*(Additional invocations)*_____

Conclusion. Loving Father, you are a God of tenderness and compassion, slow to anger and always ready to forgive. Accept our Lenten efforts at penance, and bring us in joy to the glorious day of Easter. We make our prayer through Christ our Lord.

ADDITIONAL INVITATION TO COMMUNION:

Behold Christ, whose cross reconciles us to the Father!

PRAYER AFTER COMMUNION:

In the Gospel we heard Jesus saying: "Your Father who sees all that is done in secret will reward you." Let us pray that this Eucharist will strengthen our resolve to seek God in prayer, and to share our material goods in fasting and almsgiving.

First Sunday of Lent

THEME: THE GOOD NEWS

INTRODUCTION:
Throughout history God prepared his people for a sort of good news that would shake the world to its foundations. That Good News was a person: Jesus Christ, a man like us in all things but sin. Through Jesus' death and resurrection, God has renewed the covenant he made with all mankind in the days of Noah. Such is also the Good News Christians proclaim to the world.

INVITATION TO PENITENTIAL RITE:
The Good News of Christ is convincing only if we are willing to stake our very lives on it. Let us reflect for a moment on the ways our lives have contradicted the Gospel's call to faith and repentance.

FORM C: *(Optional invocations)*
Though you were innocent, you died for our sins: Lord, have mercy.
Though you were Lord, you became the servant of all: Christ . . .
Though you were put to death, you rose to life: Lord . . .

OPENING PRAYER:
Let us pray that we may hear the Good News faithfully and show forth its power by the quality of our lives.

READINGS:
1) **Gn. 9:8-15.** The early Christians saw two important realities in the story of Noah: God's promise of universal salvation through a covenant with all mankind; and a symbol of the saving waters of Baptism.

2) **1 Pt. 3:18-22.** Our second reading from the first letter of Peter, sees, in the salvation of Noah, a symbol of our salvation through Baptism.

3) **Mk. 1:12-15.** Jesus begins to preach the Good News, and asks his hearers to repent and believe.

HOMILY NOTES:
● We are all hoping for good news, whether successful exam results, the obtaining of a new job or a raise in pay, or the return home of a friend or one of the family. The "Gospel" means Good News. It is the greatest news of all, the news that God loves us. He proved in the hard reality of Jesus' suffering and death that death is not the end of everything but the way through to a new life as sons of God.

- When Jesus returned from the desert and began his mission, he proclaimed the "Good News." What did this mean? That the time had come for a new relationship between man and God, that we are to call God Father and all men brothers. In Christ we are now sons of God, and must live as such.

- The Church is meant to be a sign to all of man's destiny. Is it? Are we, in fact, spreading the Good News by our lives? So many people today are searching for the meaning of life. They will only discover it if they experience God's love when they meet Christians, if they see in the Christian community what human life is meant to be.

- We must be open to the Holy Spirit so that God's love may penetrate everything we do, and our very lives will communicate the Good News to others.

GENERAL INTERCESSIONS:

Invitation: Conversion to the Lord is not a momentary feeling, but the rugged process of a lifetime. Let us pray that God will change our hearts and deepen our faith in the Good News of Christ. Our response is: **LORD, INCREASE OUR FAITH.**

1. That this Lenten season may produce in us a more sincere effort to model our lives on the pattern of Christ, we pray to the Lord.

2. That we may put the welfare of others above our personal ambition for success and advancement, we . . .

3. That we may accept our responsibility to see that justice is accorded the poor and defenseless, we . . .

4. For those who suffer the anguish of mental illness, we . . .

5. For those who are afflicted with crippling diseases, and for their families, we . . .

*(Additional invocations)*_____

Conclusion: Father, our efforts to live as Jesus lived are often weak and insincere. Increase our faith in the Good News of your Son, and change our hearts by the power of your Spirit. We ask this through Christ our Lord.

ADDITIONAL INVITATION TO COMMUNION:

Behold Christ, put to death in the flesh, but raised up in the Spirit!

PRAYER AFTER COMMUNION:

"Repent and believe the Good News." Let us pray that all of us who have tasted the one bread may encourage one another in our common efforts at interior renewal.

Second Sunday of Lent

THEME: OUR TRANSFIGURATION

INTRODUCTION:
The transfiguration of Jesus reveals something significant about the future of man and his world. All of creation is destined for a transfiguration which will make it radiant with God's presence and his love. The resurrection of Christ has already begun this transformation by abolishing the power of sin and death.

INVITATION TO PENITENTIAL RITE:
Let us prepare ourselves to meet the Lord of glory in this Mass by purifying our hearts of attachment to self-centered ways of thinking and acting.

FORM C: *(Optional invocations)*
When we are at the point of death, your promise gives us life: Lord, have mercy.

When we are weary and despairing, your presence gives us hope: Christ . . .

When we are overwhelmed by doubt, your passion gives us courage: Lord . . .

OPENING PRAYER:
Let us pray, remembering that Christ will transfigure us, too, with his glory.

READINGS:
1) **Gn. 22:1-2, 9, 10-13, 15-18.** Abraham is known as our father in faith because even when, by all human odds, God's promise seemed impossible of fulfillment, he continued to have trust.

2) **Rom. 8:31-34.** God's limitless love assures us, Paul remarks, that we shall not be condemned if we adhere to Christ.

3) **Mk. 9:2-10.** The sight of Jesus in the glory of his Lordship fills the disciples with strength to withstand the trial of his approaching passion and death.

HOMILY NOTES:
● Peter, James, and John were allowed to see the transfiguration so that they could see the glory of God for themselves, a demonstration of the glory that would be given Jesus forever at the resurrection. He wants us to share this glory, too. He wants to transfigure us, to transfigure the whole world.

● Our transfiguration is a gradual process. If we live by faith, we know what God wants of us — brotherhood, justice, love, and peace. But we are prejudiced, selfish, lazy, ready to take offense and slow to forgive.

● Abraham was called by God and was trusting enough to make his sacrifice. Today this call comes to us. Do we trust God enough to face these struggles, and sacrifice our whims and comforts and feelings of security? If we answer the call, God will transfigure us so that we can share his Son's glory and build a better world.

GENERAL INTERCESSIONS:

Invitation: No one knows what happiness God has prepared for those who love him, yet Jesus' transfiguration gives us a glimpse of this future joy. Let us pray confidently for the strength to remain faithful to Christ in spite of temptations, as we respond: **LORD, SHOW US YOUR GLORY.**

1. That the Church may lend its support to all who work to establish more humane conditions for the poor and underpriviledged, we pray to the Lord.

2. That men whose lives have been dwarfed by hatred and oppression may be transformed by our active charity, we . . .

3. That our baptismal transfiguration in Christ may light up the world with renewed faith and hope, we . . .

4. For all who use their inventive skill to transform mens' lives through medical and psychiatric research, we . . .

5. For all who have a special gift of consolation for the sick and sorrowing, we . . .

*(Additional invocations)*_____

Conclusion: Transform our lives, Father, by your merciful presence. Let us become what you have destined us to be: mature human beings who love your creation and praise you in every thought and deed. We make our prayer through Christ our Lord.

ADDITIONAL INVITATION TO COMMUNION:
Behold Jesus, who pleads for us at God's right hand!

PRAYER AFTER COMMUNION:
In today's second reading Paul said: "He not only died for us — he rose from the dead, and there at God's right hand he stands and pleads for us." Let us pray that we may leave this Mass renewed by Christ's transfiguring love and ready to work for the transformation of all creation.

Third Sunday of Lent

THEME: HONEST WORSHIP

INTRODUCTION:

There is an old proverb: "Familiarity breeds contempt." Because worship is such a familiar feature of Christian life, it is always in danger of becoming mere ritualism devoid of inner spirit. Today's liturgy reminds us that the only worship acceptable to God is that done honestly in spirit and in truth.

INVITATION TO PENITENTIAL RITE:

Let us begin this common act of praise and thanksgiving by reflecting on those times when we have allowed our worship to become an empty formalism.

FORM C: *(Optional invocations)*

Son of God, source of peace and reconciliation among brothers: Lord, have mercy.

Word of God, calling us to faith and repentance: Christ . . .

Servant of God, showing us how to worship in spirit and truth: Lord . . .

OPENING PRAYER:

Let us prepare our hearts for honest participation in this Eucharistic mystery by praying for a deeper understanding of what it means to worship in spirit and in truth.

READINGS:

1) **Ex. 20:1-17.** Sometimes we are tempted to contrast Old Testament "legalism" with New Testament love. But today's first reading from Exodus shows that love has always been essential for real obedience to God's commands.

2) **1 Cor. 1:22-25.** Paul writes that the foolishness of God is wisdom for those on the way to salvation in Christ.

3) **Jn. 2:13-25.** The true sanctuary of Christians is not a particular place, but rather the body of Jesus raised up in glory.

HOMILY NOTES:

● The first reading is about the Ten Commandments, God's basic instructions for the relationship of man to his Creator, and man to his fellows. We know that the Ten Commandments are a skeleton on which men have put flesh and sinew.

● These can be legitimate developments or they can add unnecessary details which obscure essentials, e.g., the elaborate ritual of the Temple and its dependent services of buying and selling. In the keen atmosphere of trading and bargaining, the real object, God's worship, got lost; hence Jesus' anger. He especially had the right to protest, the Son of the Father for whom the Temple was built.

● Asked for his authority, he said "destroy this Temple and in three days I will raise it up." In his risen body (the Temple destroyed and rebuilt) is our true worship of the Father. We must be careful not to load our worship with details that obscure the essential, that we are a sinful people redeemed by Christ's sacrifice.

● Through our re-presentation of this sacrifice in the Eucharist we offer true worship to the Father.

GENERAL INTERCESSIONS:

Invitation: The Gospel for today's liturgy remarks that Jesus needed no evidence about any man, since he knew what was in man's heart. If we are honest with ourselves, we realize how dependent we are on God's help to live a life worthy of our Christian calling. Let us offer honest prayer to the Father, as we respond: **LORD, CLEANSE OUR HEARTS.**

1. That the Church's worship may reflect the honesty of lives dedicated to the humble service of God and neighbor, we pray to the Lord.

2. That those who minister at the liturgy as readers, commentators, singers, and musicians may do so with joyful enthusiasm, we . . .

3. That we may conform our actions in daily life to the words we speak in worship, we . . .

4. For those in our parish who are unable to celebrate with us because of illness, we . . .

5. For those who have died recently, that they may rejoice forever in the Kingdom of God, our Father, we . . .

*(Additional invocations)*_____

Conclusion: Father, you search the heart of every man and you know our most intimate thoughts. Strengthen our hearts for more honest worship and our hands for more willing service to others, through Christ our Lord.

ADDITIONAL INVITATION TO COMMUNION:
Behold the Wisdom and Power of God!

PRAYER AFTER COMMUNION:
"God's foolishness is wiser than human wisdom, and God's weakness is stronger than human strength." Let us give thanks to the Father for calling us to share in the body of his Son, who himself is our wisdom and strength.

Fourth Sunday of Lent

THEME: GOD'S LOVING KINDNESS

INTRODUCTION:

Most of us would define "kindness" as "simply a decent, humane way of treating others." Perhaps we even think that, while we cannot love everybody deeply, we can at least be kind to them. But God's kindness is a vastly richer reality: it is a love so powerful it can raise the dead back to life and can save persons who are otherwise lost.

INVITATION TO PENITENTIAL RITE:

As we prepare to receive God's limitless kindness in this Eucharist, let us pause to reflect on the ways we make excuses to avoid sharing some of this kindness with others.

FORM C: *(Optional invocations)*

You were sent not to condemn, but to save the world: Lord, have mercy.
You showed us a new way to live through love: Christ . . .
You opened up the path to everlasting life: Lord . . .

OPENING PRAYER:

Let us pray that this Lent may bring us to a more vital faith, a more selfless generosity, and a more intimate union with Christ.

READINGS:

1) **2 Chr. 36:14-16, 19-23.** Despite Israel's sin, God is tireless in his efforts to spare his people and bring them back from exile.

2) **Eph. 2:4-10.** Paul is lyrical in his description of what God has done for believers in Christ: he has given us life, raised us up, and seated us with his Son in heaven.

3) **Jn. 3:14-21.** God's relation to the world is not one of anger, but of love — strong love that brings salvation to all who believe in Jesus.

HOMILY NOTES:

● The reading from the book of Chronicles tells us of one of the many occasions when Israel turned away from God. Time and again his messengers were ignored, his prophets persecuted.

• The outcome of this foolishness for Israel was an experience which, because of its terrible consequences, prepared and made sensitive the mind of the people so that God could approach yet again with his love and forgiveness. And God went so far as to send his Son so that we might recognize the lengths he would go to show his love.

• The realization of God's love, of his unfailing pursuit of each of his creatures, should help us see that his watchfulness is not that of one waiting with an all-seeing eye to spot our faults and failures. He wants to forget immediately the wrong and encourage us to start afresh, assured of his love.

GENERAL INTERCESSIONS:

Invitation: God's loving kindness is not a restricted commodity: it is waiting for us whenever we call upon him in faith. Let us approach the Lord with bold confidence, as we pray: **LORD, SAVE YOUR PEOPLE.**

1. That the Church may become truly a sacrament of God's love and truth in the world, we pray to the Lord.

2. That sinners may seek healing through God's forgiving mercy in the sacrament of reconciliation, we . . .

3. That this Lent may direct the hearts of men toward peace and life, and away from war and death, we . . .

4. For those whom imprisonment has maimed and hardened, that the mercy of God may lighten their suffering, we . . .

5. For more effective and charitable ways of helping those addicted to drugs, we . . .

*(Additional invocations)*_____

Conclusion: Time and time again, Father, you have stretched out your hand to save us, when we were at the point of falling. For all your great goodness we give you thanks, and ask that, in our lives, mercy may temper our demands for justice. We ask this through Christ our Lord.

ADDITIONAL INVITATION TO COMMUNION:
Behold the Savior of the world!

PRAYER AFTER COMMUNION:
In John's Gospel we heard: "God loved the world so much that he gave his only Son." Let us pause for a moment and be thankful for the gift of Eucharist, which renews in us the love God has for his creation.

Fifth Sunday of Lent

THEME: THROUGH DEATH TO LIFE

INTRODUCTION:

Nothing seems more brutally final than death. Anyone who has ever experienced a war, or visited a hospital ward for the terminally ill knows that death is a devastating, powerful event. But the Christian does not see death as the ultimate finality; he sees it as the passage to a glorious life with the risen Lord.

INVITATION TO PENITENTIAL RITE:

My friends, the only death that is final for a Christian is his baptismal death to sin. Let us examine ourselves to see how often we have clung to sin by avoiding Christ's life in the sacraments, in the Scriptures, and in the lives of our brothers.

FORM C: *(Optional invocations)*

You create in us new hearts to know and love you: Lord, have mercy.
You open our ears to hear your Word: Christ . . .
You grant us new eyes to see in your death the source of life: Lord . . .

OPENING PRAYER:

Let us offer prayer in silence for a moment after the example of Jesus, who prayed in silent tears to the Father.

READINGS:

1) **Jer. 31:31-34.** Through the prophet Jeremiah, God promises his people a new covenant which will be written on human hearts.

2) **Heb. 5:7-9.** Christ offered prayer in silent tears to the Father who could save him from death — and his prayer was heard.

3) **Jn. 12:20-33.** Just as the seed dies to bring forth a harvest of wheat, Jesus' death will result in a harvest of life for men.

HOMILY NOTES:

● As Jeremiah tells us in the first reading, something had gone wrong with man's alliance with God. The people thought it bound God to them; in reality, it bound men to God.

● God said that he would give men a new law to live by, would "write it in their hearts." We know what this law is, Christ's law of love, which he came to show us.

- Keeping this law involves a death, death to selfishness. We must be prepared to lose our life in this world, lose promotion, security or social esteem, if these things stand in the way of service of Christ and witness to his truth.

- Out of this "death" to self comes a new life Christ offers. The message he came to proclaim resulted in his death at the hands of men; but, because of his fidelity, the Father raised him to a new life. By our fidelity to Christ and his law of love, we will be receivers of his new life, too.

GENERAL INTERCESSIONS:

Invitation: The second reading for today's Mass reminded us that Christ prayed earnestly for the strength to face death. In their own way, our pains and disappointments are daily deaths. So let us ask for fortitude to face them, as we respond: **LORD, GIVE US COURAGE.**

1. That those who suffer persecution in Christ's name may be given the grace to withstand their trials, we pray to the Lord.

2. That we may participate in Christ's passion by sharing the hunger and thirst of the poor, we . . .

3. That Christians may witness to the fact that there is more to life than the pursuit of success and the accumulation of wealth, we . . .

4. For innocent children who experience the living death of hunger and disease, we . . .

*(Additional invocations)*_____

Conclusion: Father of our Lord Jesus, give us strength to mend broken hearts and shattered lives. Help us become living centers of your presence in the world, so that all men may know that death is not the absolute end, but the new beginning of abundant life. We ask this through Christ our Lord.

ADDITIONAL INVITATION TO COMMUNION:
Behold the Lord who draws all men to himself!

PRAYER AFTER COMMUNION:
John puts these words on the lips of Christ: "When I am lifted up from the earth, I shall draw all men to myself." Let us pray that, as we have been drawn into unity around this table, all men may be united in the life which flows from the cross of Christ.

43

Passion Sunday (Palm Sunday)

THEME: THE DISASTER OF THE CROSS

INTRODUCTION:

At the heart of Christianity there stands a colossal paradox: the cross of Jesus. At one and the same time, the cross speaks of disaster and triumph, despair and hope, death and life. St. Paul remarked that to many this cross seems like utter madness. But for those who believe, the cross promises a life fuller and richer than anything we can imagine.

INVITATION TO PENITENTIAL RITE:

As we prepare for the week of Christ's passion and victory, let us recall how often we have sought a comfortable Christianity free from crosses and free from any real personal dedication.

FORM C: *(Optional invocations)*

Your passion and cross reconciles us with the Father: Lord, have mercy.

Your suffering and anguish renews our faith: Christ . . .

Your victory over death restores us to life: Lord . . .

OPENING PRAYER:

Let us pray that the cross of Christ may be for us neither scandal nor embarrassment, but hope for a new life.

READINGS:

1) **Is. 50:4-7.** The Suffering Servant is described by Isaiah as the obedient disciple of the Lord.

2) **Phil. 2:6-11.** In our second reading we listen to a hymn about Jesus, the humble Servant who accepted even death on a cross and was exalted by the Father.

3) **Mk. 14:1—15:47.** Mark gives us one of the earliest accounts of the passion, trial, and death of Jesus.

HOMILY NOTES:

● Today in her liturgy, the Church calls us to relive the Passion of Jesus. The Gospel version is from Mark, the companion of Peter, whose personal experience figures so poignantly in this early confused account of the dramatic failure in human terms of the Messiah's life.

● Christ chided Peter and his companions, "Are you asleep? You should be awake, praying not to be put to the test." But they could find no answer as to why they had failed him. The answer lies in our inability to do things well: our ineptness, our imperfection.

44

• It is this imperfection, this handicapped quality that God the Son embraced in the Incarnation. In becoming man he took on weakness in the quality of his life even though he was innocent of personal sin. But the goodness of Jesus, which was recognized by the centurion at the foot of the cross, brought Christ in human terms to his death at the hands of the jealous, angry and shocked men who turned on him much as we might do in the same situation.

• His death was inevitable in human terms because he persisted in his teaching which challenged the entrenched leadership. But it was also in God's plan to save men. Jesus suffers death as one of us — and from that death the Father raised him, and made him Lord and Savior, bringing life out of death.

GENERAL INTERCESSIONS:

Invitation: Although the cross is a symbol of violence and death, it has become for Christians the supreme sign of God's enormous love. Let us pray that such love will bring healing to the wounds of a world in need of unity and hope. Our response is: **LORD, WE PRAISE YOUR CROSS.**

1. That the Church may be renewed in holiness by the mystery of Christ's cross, we pray to the Lord.

2. That the cross may become the effective sign of reconciliation among all men, we . . .

3. That our own sufferings may not lead us to self-pity, but rather to deeper union with Christ and with all who are afflicted, we . . .

4. That we may be forgiven for the times our selfishness has inflicted hardship and pain on others, we . . .

5. For those who work to bring relief to the sick and the dying, we . . .

*(Additional invocations)*_____

Conclusion: Your boundless love, Father, has saved the world through the cross of your Son. Let us become faithful witnesses of that cross through lives that are patient in sufferings, generous in service, and courageous in action. We make our prayer through Christ our Lord.

ADDITIONAL INVITATION TO COMMUNION:

Behold the Lord whose cross reconciles all things in heaven and on earth!

PRAYER AFTER COMMUNION:

In today's reading from Philippians we heard: ". . . every tongue should acclaim Jesus Christ as Lord, to the glory of God the Father." As we go forth from this Eucharist, let us pray that our share in the cross of Jesus may lead us to the joy of his paschal Lordship.

Holy Thursday

THEME: THE NEW PASSOVER

INTRODUCTION:

Throughout the Old Testament the sharing of a meal had sacred significance. But Israelites were more intensely conscious of divine providence and communion in the Passover meal, a feast which celebrated Israel's deliverance and identity as a chosen people. Jesus' final meal with his disciples inaugurated a new Passover. The bread and wine of the paschal supper signified Jesus' body and blood given up in sacrifice and destined for the glory of resurrection. This is the supper we share at every Eucharist.

INVITATION TO PENITENTIAL RITE:

To share in Christ's supper without being reconciled to one another is to falsify our worship. Let us pause to follow the example of Jesus by forgiving one another from the depths of our hearts.

FORM C: *(Optional invocations)*

We praise you for the Bread and the Cup that make us a people: Lord, have mercy.
We bless you for the death that brings us life: Christ . . .
We glorify you for the resurrection that renews all creation: Lord . . .

OPENING PRAYER:

Let us pray that we will recognize Christ in this breaking of bread by recognizing him also in our brothers and sisters.

READINGS:

1) **Ex. 12:1-8, 11-14.** The Passover meal was a family celebration rich in symbolic meaning. As a Jew, Jesus would have been thoroughly familiar with the traditional Passover, and it was this meal which he transformed by making it the sign of his own sacrifice.

2) **1 Cor. 11:23-26.** Paul hands on to the Corinthians the tradition he received about the Lord's Supper: the broken bread and cup of wine proclaim Christ's saving death.

3) **Jn. 13:1-15.** On the eve of his betrayal and death Jesus continues to behave as a servant by washing the disciples' feet.

HOMILY NOTES:

● Christ chose to offer the sacrifice of himself in the context of the annual Passover celebration. In accordance with the ritual, he described how the broken bread was his own body and the cup of thanksgiving was his own blood that would, like the blood of the

Passover lamb, free us from slavery and would as well deliver us from all that separates us from God.

● Jesus commanded us to do this in memory of him. This is not a simple remembering, but a re-presentation of those acts of Christ which achieve our passover into the presence of God.

● As we take part in this mystery, St. Paul reminds us of the love and mutual service we must have if we are worthily to proclaim the death of the Lord until he comes. Jesus himself showed us how to serve when he took on himself a job usually done by a servant; namely, the washing of the feet of the assembled guests.

GENERAL INTERCESSIONS:

Invitation: In washing his disciples' feet Jesus revealed that the Eucharist signifies more than personal nourishment; it also demands self-forgetting love. Let us pray for an active love that is not afraid to show its concern for the people who need us. Our response is: **LIVE IN US, LORD.**

1. For all who serve God's People as pastors, especially those who are lonely and forgotten, we pray to the Lord.

2. That wealthy nations may share their abundance with people who go to bed hungry each night, we . . .

3. That the voice of peacemakers may find a favorable reception in nations torn apart by war and civil discontent, we . . .

4. That, on this day especially, all Christian believers may grow in the desire for unity around the Lord's table, we . . .

5. For our Jewish brothers, as they begin to prepare for the celebration of Passover, we . . .

*(Additional invocations)*_____

Conclusion: On this day, Father, we are grateful for simple gifts: for light and water, for the rough beauty of rock and wood, for the strength of hands ready to serve. But we thank you especially for the bread that is Christ's body and the wine that is our covenant with you in his blood. Make us worthy, Father, of these and all your gifts, for we make our prayer through Christ our Lord.

ADDITIONAL INVITATION TO COMMUNION:
Behold Christ, our New Passover!

PRAYER AFTER COMMUNION:
"He had always loved those who were his own in the world, but now he showed how perfect his love was." Let us pray for a love that seeks fulfillment in a life of total dedication to Christ present among his people.

47

Easter Sunday

THEME: NEW LIFE

INTRODUCTION:

To the question "What is life?" there are probably as many answers as there are living persons. But St. Paul touched the heart of the matter in a single word: Life is Christ. For Christians Jesus Christ is a new life because he alone conquered the destructive power of death and rose to live in a people. We are that people, living Christ's life through Baptism, eating and drinking with him now that he is risen from the dead.

INVITATION TO PENITENTIAL RITE:

Today our first reading has Peter saying: ". . . all who believe in Jesus will have their sins forgiven through his name." We sometimes forget that God forgives us more readily than we forgive ourselves; so let us ask pardon for the times we have not trusted in his mercy.

FORM C: *(Optional invocations)*

Risen Lord, fountain of living water in Baptism: Lord, have mercy.
Risen Lord, Giver of the Spirit of holiness: Christ . . .
Risen Lord, food and drink for us in the Eucharist: Lord . . .

OPENING PRAYER:

On this day which the Lord has made, let us pray for a life so new and dynamic that it will shatter every form of human imprisonment and free all men for witnessing to Christ's Lordship.

READINGS:

1) **Acts 10:34, 37-43.** In our first reading from Acts, Peter comments that he is a witness to Jesus' resurrection because he has eaten and drunk with the risen Lord.

2) **Col. 3:1-4.** If someone were to tell us we had died, we would probably not believe him. But Paul tells us today that, when Christ died, we died in him and now we live his risen life.

3) **Jn. 20:1-9.** For Peter and John the empty tomb reveals the meaning of the Scriptures: Christ has risen and poured new life over all creation.

HOMILY NOTES:

● As God's children we are co-heirs with Christ and share his inheritance. Christ came to make us fully alive, to make it possible for us to realize our capacities to the utmost.

- The resurrection is the natural climax to Christ's life and death. Christ was so perfectly attuned to God that nothing could separate him from God; he and his Father are one. Our vocation, too, is to be perfectly at one with God and thus to become more fully human.

- We achieve this by taking on the rights and responsibilities of the new Christian life. This implies death to sin, a wholehearted love of God and neighbor, acceptance of new standards, and single-mindedness.

- Our aim is to be so caught up in Christ that we see, think, feel, and act as Christ; that we become other Christs. We then share not only his suffering but also his glory.

GENERAL INTERCESSIONS:

Invitation: Jesus, the New Man, offers every human being the possibility of being united with his paschal mystery. Conscious of our common human vocation to life in Christ, let us offer prayer for the needs of all, as we respond: **LORD, GIVE US NEW LIFE.**

1. That all men may become aware of their interdependence, and their responsibility for promoting the mature spiritual dignity of every living person, we pray to the Lord.

2. That governments may work for a human society built on respect for both common good and individual freedom, we . . .

3. That the Church may become truly a church of the poor, sharing the human riddles of sorrow and death, and proclaiming the hope that comes from Jesus' resurrection, we . . .

4. For all the newly baptized, that they may find in us, their brothers and sisters, constant support and encouragement, we . . .

5. For all who live in fear of death, that the rising of Jesus may calm their fear and fill them with peace, we . . .

*(Additional invocations)*_____

Conclusion: Everything that lives and breathes gives you praise, Father, for you are a God who loves life. We rejoice today in the rising of your Son, and we pray that his new life may provide the impulse for increasing unity among men. We make our prayer through Christ our Lord.

ADDITIONAL INVITATION TO COMMUNION:
Behold the Risen Lord: He is your Life!

PRAYER AFTER COMMUNION:
"We have eaten and drunk with him after his resurrection from the dead." Let us pray that our communion in the risen Jesus may lead us to a new respect for the mystery of everything that is fully alive.

Second Sunday of Easter

THEME: CHRISTIAN JOY

INTRODUCTION:
For the early Christians Easter was the original feast day, and each Sunday was dedicated to the renewed, joyful celebration of Christ's paschal mystery. Such was and is the source of a Christian's optimism. While Christians do not discount the sober realism of human suffering and tragedy, they cannot help breaking into praise of the Lord, who has brought life out of death, and joy out of sadness.

INVITATION TO PENITENTIAL RITE:
We will hear in today's first reading that Christian joy results from unity of heart and soul. Let us reflect on those occasions when our quarrelsome demands have disrupted the unity of family, church and world.

FORM C: *(Optional invocations)*
Rising from the dead, you poured joy on all the earth: Lord, have mercy.

Ascending to your Father, you gave gifts of freedom to men: Christ . . .

Sending your Spirit, you made us a people united in heart and soul: Lord . . .

OPENING PRAYER:
Let us pray that we may find our joy in giving unity where it has been lost and love where it has never been experienced.

READINGS:
1) **Acts 4:32-35.** Our first reading provides a description of the early Christian community united in heart, soul and material goods. This model remains a vital challenge to all communities which call themselves Christian.

2) **1 Jn. 5:1-6.** Becoming a child begotten of God means having faith in Jesus Christ. This faith will mature into love which overcomes everything opposed to the truth.

3) **Jn. 20:19-31.** The first greeting of the risen Lord to his disciples is one of peace. That peace is made perfect by the Holy Spirit, who pledges the forgiveness of our sins.

HOMILY NOTES:
● Real joy comes with knowledge that we are loved and can love in return.

- The early Christians had a heightened sense of responsibility to the community around them. Acts of sharing, helping, looking for opportunities to serve were part of everyday life.

- There are no fewer opportunities today for us to follow their example, but the needs may be more subtle. We must serve in the joyful knowledge of an unseen but risen and present Christ. He must be for us a source of gladness as he was to the apostles in the upper room pondering on the mysterious events of the first Easter.

- Our faith must support a profound knowledge of Christ's presence, not the "seeing is believing" attitude of Thomas. Our joyful response must come from a well-spring of Christ's life in each of us.

GENERAL INTERCESSIONS:

Invitation: Christ's resurrection revealed that he is the source and goal of all human progress and history. Let us pray that the yearning all men experience for a sense of personal dignity and value may be brought to fulfillment in Christ. Our response is: **HEAR US, LORD OF GLORY.**

1. That the Church may remain faithful to its basic mission to re-establish all things in and through Christ, we pray to the Lord.

2. That political and ecclesiastical governments may always seek to serve the needs of persons and not those of powerful pressure groups, we . . .

3. That we may work for the full recognition of the fundamental human rights of freedom and personal conscience, we . . .

4. For persons whose lives have been mutilated by coercion and subhuman living conditions, we . . .

5. For persons who have never known the joy of friendship and trust, we . . .

*(Additional invocations)*_____

Conclusion: Father, the whole of creation longs to see your glory and to feel your loving presence. Renew in us a profound sense of the dignity and value we have as your children, and raise us up to a new life of friendship with you. We make our prayer through Christ our Lord.

ADDITIONAL INVITATION TO COMMUNION:

Behold Christ, risen to fill his disciples with the joy that comes from peace.

PRAYER AFTER COMMUNION:

"The disciples were filled with joy when they saw the Lord, and he said to them again: 'Peace be with you.' " Let us pray, asking Christ to fulfill the longing every man has for a happiness which cannot be destroyed by human weakness or malice.

51

Third Sunday of Easter

THEME: THE FORGIVENESS OF SIN

INTRODUCTION:

True peace seems to be the one thing everybody wants and nobody has. But Jesus' Easter promise to men is a peace that grows out of hearts which know how to forgive and how to be forgiven. This kind of peace is free for the asking, but it demands the risk of allowing God's inventive love to take us outside ourselves and into the lives of others.

INVITATION TO PENITENTIAL RITE:

Let us pause to reflect on the words we say in the Lord's Prayer: "Forgive us . . . as we forgive those who trespass against us." These words indicate that the way to experience forgiveness is to start giving it to others. Let us do just that.

FORM C: *(Optional invocations)*

You are the Servant whom the Father has glorified: Lord, have mercy.

You are the Sacrifice that takes away our sins: Christ . . .

You are the Peacemaker who offers reconciliation to all men: Lord . . .

OPENING PRAYER:

Let us pray, asking Christ to show us both how to forgive and how to accept forgiveness.

READINGS:

1) **Acts 3:13-15, 17-19.** Peter speaks to the people and tells them the God of Abraham, Isaac and Jacob has raised up the Jesus whom they have disowned and crucified.

2) **1 Jn. 2:1-5.** God's love is not the exclusive privilege of a few persons. In our second reading, John tells us that Christ's sacrifice brings forgiveness not only to us but to all the world.

3) **Lk. 24:35-48.** The risen Lord opens the minds of his disciples to understand the meaning of the Scriptures which prophesy his suffering, death, and resurrection.

HOMILY NOTES:

● "In his name, repentance for the forgiveness of sins would be preached to all the nations." "Peace be with you." In the reading from Luke we are emphasizing the point made by John "that Christ comes to take our sins away, and not only ours but those of the whole world."

52

• The message we have to proclaim is that forgiveness of our sins is there for the asking as we repent. The word used for repentance, in the original Greek, means "a turning inside out." This is partly what we mean by education; we are drawn out, we can change ourselves if we are encouraged, if we know that we are loved.

• This, then, is the great news: God loves us and has forgiven us our sins. We must turn ourselves inside out and accept this, do something about it. If we do, we will find ourselves changing under his influence; he will, through his power, gradually lessen the effects of sin in us. We will begin to know the truth that, when we open ourselves to God's will, we are cooperating with Love itself.

GENERAL INTERCESSIONS:

Invitation: The Gospel does not conspire with our preference for easy and comfortable religion. Rather, it makes sturdy demands on us. It requires the forgiveness of those who injure us, it asks us to substitute love for cruelty and peace for violence. Let us ask God's help in fulfilling the Gospel law of love, as we pray: **LORD, TEACH US TO FORGIVE.**

1. That men who differ in social, political and religious allegiances may grow in reverence and respect for one another, we pray to the Lord.

2. That, since God alone searches men's hearts, we may refrain from passing hasty judgments on the lives of our neighbors, we . . .

3. For those whom prejudice has deprived of access to better educational and cultural opportunities, we . . .

4. For persons whom we find especially difficult to love and forgive, we . . .

5. For persons whose lives have been emotionally crippled by cruelty and hatred, we . . .

(Additional invocations) _____

Conclusion: Father, when your Son was about to die, he sought forgiveness for those who tormented him. Forgive us now for the times we have done injury to the members of Christ's body through our refusal to pardon. We make this prayer through the same Christ our Lord.

ADDITIONAL INVITATION TO COMMUNION:

Behold our Advocate with the Father — Jesus who is just!

PRAYER AFTER COMMUNION:

The First Letter of John reminded us that "if anyone should sin, we have our Advocate with the Father, Jesus Christ who is just." Let us pray that our sharing in the one Bread of Life may be the sign of our mutual forgiveness and reconciliation.

Fourth Sunday of Easter

THEME: BELONGING TO CHRIST

INTRODUCTION:

For Israel, circumcision was the physical sign of belonging to a covenant-community. After Jesus's death and resurrection, the New Testament writers used a number of bold images to express the same notion of belonging, personally and communally, to God. They spoke of being clothed with Christ, of having the same Spirit that raised Jesus from death, of being Christ's body. All these images reflect a single reality: through Baptism we were marked forever as belonging to Christ.

INVITATION TO PENITENTIAL RITE:

Sometimes we deceive ourselves by imagining that the greatest freedom lies in having obligations to nobody. As we begin this Mass, let us recall the ways we have made excuses to shirk our responsibilities as baptized members of Christ's body.

FORM C: *(Optional invocations)*

We are your members, because we died and rose with you in Baptism: Lord, have mercy.

We are your brothers, because we share the same Spirit that raised you from death: Christ . . .

We are your people, because we eat and drink from your table: Lord . . .

OPENING PRAYER:

As a people that belongs to Christ through Baptism, let us open our hearts to his Word in this liturgy.

READINGS:

1) **Acts. 4:8-12.** What Peter said to the crowds in Jerusalem must have sounded incredibly shocking: Jesus, crucified like a common criminal, is the sole source of salvation for men.

2) **1 Jn. 3:1-2.** John praises the Father's lavish love and looks toward a future time when we ourselves shall be like God.

3) **Jn. 10:11-18.** In biblical language "to know" refers to deep, inter-personal communion. Today's Gospel reveals how profound Christ's relation to his people is: he knows them and they know him.

HOMILY NOTES:

● In the Gospel Jesus tells us that he knows us individually. We received our names at Baptism in the name of Jesus. We belong to him. As John says, we are already his children.

● This is not just a casual acquaintance. Peter describes what Jesus has done for us: "By him only do we stand up healthy, healed from our sins." But in the Gospel we hear not only "I know my own," but also "mine know me." Through his love he has made himself known to us.

● On us, therefore, lies the duty of making him known to those "not of this fold," of telling them of the Savior who has laid down his life that we may live.

GENERAL INTERCESSIONS:

Invitation: Belonging to Christ means more than obeying Church rules and muttering a few prayers now and then. It means that Christ must permeate every aspect of life: our private thoughts, our work, our values, our priorities, our view of society. Let us pray, asking that Christ may saturate us with his own life and Spirit, as we respond: **LORD, BE OUR LIGHT.**

1. That in union with its Lord, the Church may avoid seeking comfortable securities, so that it may share the ordinary aspirations and trials of human life, we pray to the Lord.

2. That the Church may consistently voice its opposition to the subtle forms of exploitation that result in the use of persons as tools of profit, we . . .

3. That the Gospel may continue to console the sorrowing and disturb the consciences of the complacent, we . . .

4. That we may learn to love as Christ loved — freely, deeply, without counting the cost, we . . .

5. For those who suffer, especially the lonely and the aged, because we have been too preoccupied to care about them, we . . .

*(Additional invocations)*_____

Conclusion: Father, we belong to you as a people bought with the great price of Jesus' blood. Make us conscious of our dignity and responsibility as Christians, and help us strive to build a world united in faith, hope and love, through Christ our Lord.

ADDITIONAL INVITATION TO COMMUNION:
Behold the Lord Jesus, whose name brings salvation!

PRAYER AFTER COMMUNION:
"Of all names in the world given to men, this is the only one by which we can be saved." Let us pray for courage to profess the name of Jesus even in moments of doubt and temptation.

Fifth Sunday of Easter

THEME: LOVE MEANS ACTION

INTRODUCTION:

People in love not only enjoy each other's presence; they also seek to pool their time and effort towards building a deeper, more mature love. If love remains a purely intellectual affair, it soon grows cold and disappears. In today's second reading John will remind Christians that real love for Christ cannot be all words; it has to be active, it has to do things. It is this active doing which distinguishes genuine love from mere infatuation or deceit.

INVITATION TO PENITENTIAL RITE:

Brothers and sisters, as we prepare to celebrate God's active love for us in the Eucharist, let us honestly admit that at times our love has been much talk and little action.

FORM C: *(Optional invocations)*

By speaking the truth, you showed us the commandments of life: Lord, have mercy.

By loving actively, you taught us to lay down our lives for one another: Christ . . .

By rising from death, you filled us with the Holy Spirit: Lord . . .

OPENING PRAYER:

Let us pray for a love that is expressive, that seeks to lift up the unloved and the unwanted.

READINGS:

1) **Acts 9:26-31.** One of the most painful situations Paul faced after his conversion was the mistrust of the other disciples in Jerusalem. It was Barnabas' efforts at reconciliation which finally legitimated Paul's standing as an apostle of the risen Christ.

2) **1 Jn. 3:18-24.** We sometimes ask how we can be sure we really know and love Christ. In our second reading John supplies an answer: we know we are living the truth if we have a lively love for one another.

3) **Jn. 15:1-8.** In the Gospel Jesus tells us that, if his word remains in us, we can ask for anything and receive it.

HOMILY NOTES:

● Barnabas was a great person, generous, "a good man filled with the Holy Spirit and with faith." After Paul left Damascus, he visited Jerusalem and found it hostile. Barnabas took charge, soothed and sorted out the situation, introduced and explained.

- Barnabas has a lesson for us. Love is not "just words or mere talk, but something real and active." Our love for other people must be lively, fruitful in action. If it is, then we can be certain that we "are children of truth"; that is, we are living our lives in accordance with God's will. Then we are branches of the true vine, with God living in us and ourselves in him.

- Even if our consciences do not reproach us, we will find that God as judge is both more acute and more lenient than our consciences, so long as we show a real love for other people.

GENERAL INTERCESSIONS:

Invitation: Sometimes we allow our view of life to shrink into the narrow limits of workaday drudgery and routine. But the Gospel vision of life is richer, more colorful. Christ has promised a more creative life to those who remain faithful to his words; so let us confidently pray: **LORD, ENRICH OUR LIVES.**

1. That as God's People we may contribute actively toward the development of those human potentials which can transform this earth into a cleaner, more satisfying place to live, we pray to the Lord.

2. That, by fostering the growth of human personalities, the Church may open up to man the deepest truth about himself, we . . .

3. That our presentation of the Gospel challenge through catechetical instruction may break out of dullness and take on the colorful variety of life itself, we . . .

4. That our cheerfulness may bring light to those who feel lonely and cheated by life, we . . .

5. For those who struggle to enhance the quality of human existence through their work in education, literature, and the arts, we . . .

*(Additional invocations)*_____

Conclusion: You have given us a world, Father, teeming with life and color. Increase our awareness of your presence in all things, and enrich our lives by the creating Spirit of your love, through Christ our Lord.

ADDITIONAL INVITATION TO COMMUNION:
Behold the holy vine of David, whose branches we are.

PRAYER AFTER COMMUNION:
"I am the vine, you are the branches . . . cut off from me you can do nothing." One with Christ in this sacrament of unity, let us pledge ourselves to love actively, relying not on our own resources but on his support.

Sixth Sunday of Easter

THEME: GOD'S LOVE FOR MAN

INTRODUCTION:

"Love" can be a tricky word. It has been used to justify everything from the buying and selling of human bodies to military atrocities committed "in the national interest." But one sort of love is sure and unfailing: God's love for man. This love was revealed most vividly when Jesus laid down his life for his friends. We are his friends if we are willing to risk loving as he did.

INVITATION TO PENITENTIAL RITE:

God's love has the power to make acceptable persons whom conventional society would label as outcast and disreputable. Let us repent of the ways we have allowed social pressure to prejudice us against people whose life-styles differ from our own.

FORM C: *(Optional invocations)*

You called us friends and revealed the Father's love: Lord, have mercy.

You commissioned us as witnesses to your truth: Christ . . .

You consoled us by pouring your Spirit into our hearts: Lord . . .

OPENING PRAYER:

Let us pray for an honest discipleship modeled on Jesus' self-sacrificing love.

READINGS:

1) **Acts 10:25-26, 34-35, 44-48.** Almost immediately the first Christians were faced with a controversy about whether the Gospel message was meant also for non-Jews. In this passage from Acts, Peter claims that Christ's message and his gift of the Holy Spirit are intended for men of every nationality.

2) **1 Jn. 4:7-10.** Our second reading stresses a favorite theme of the paschal season: God can be known only through love of neighbor.

3) **Jn. 15:9-17.** Today we hear another section from Jesus' farewell homily at the Last Supper. Once again he calls his disciples to an obedient love.

HOMILY NOTES:

● We realize today that the Holy Spirit is at work in all men, even if they do not know Christ or belong to the Church. Any man who seeks what is true and good is truly seeking God.

● St. John tells us: "He who loves is born of God and knows God. He who does not love does not know God; for God is love." The Christian life is really very simple. It is not a question of keeping rules and regulations or of worrying about our spiritual state.

● A man about to die means what he says, especially when talking to his friends. Our Lord, the night before he died, gave us the simple command to love one another as he loved us. Doing this, with all that it implies in service to our family, our neighbor, to those in need, we shall find God and find happiness. We shall also be a sign to our fellowmen who are searching for God.

GENERAL INTERCESSIONS:

Invitation: We have the privilege of offering common prayer because we have been united in one faith, one Lord, and one Baptism. Let us, then, pray in our hearts for the needs of God's Church and his world. Our response is: **HEAR US, RISEN LORD.**

1. For all who have come to this church today to offer praise and thanksgiving to the Father, we pray to the Lord.

2. For those who hunger and thirst for that peace which the world cannot give, we . . .

3. For those who mourn, that they may receive comfort in their sorrow, we . . .

4. That, as disciples of a Christ who was poor, we may share the griefs and anxieties of those who live in poverty, we . . .

5. That this whole day may be brightened by the presence of Christ, who is our light and salvation, we . . .

*(Additional invocations)*_____

Conclusion: Lord Jesus Christ, you promised to be present wherever two or three are gathered in your name. Hear our common prayers and, in your mercy, fulfill also those needs we do not know how to express in words. We ask this of you who live and reign with the Father and the Holy Spirit, now and forever.

ADDITIONAL INVITATION TO COMMUNION:
Behold the Lord who laid down his life for his friends.

PRAYER AFTER COMMUNION:
"This is my commandment: love one another as I have loved you." Rooted in love through the Eucharistic mystery, let us pray that our actions this coming week will serve to build up Christ's body in faith and in hope.

59

Ascension

THEME: HOPE

INTRODUCTION:

The Ascension is not a farewell feast; it does not lament Jesus' absence. Rather, it celebrates the new way Christ becomes present to his people through the gift of the Spirit. Ascension and Pentecost are two sides of the same mystery — Jesus is exalted as Lord of his Church, which lives and grows because of his indwelling Spirit. Such is the source of our faith and our hope.

INVITATION TO PENITENTIAL RITE:

In today's second reading Paul reminds us that, as Church, we are the very body of Christ — a body that brings light and hope to the world. Let us ask forgiveness for the ways our pessimism has crushed the hope and spirit of others.

FORM C: *(Optional invocations)*

We praise you as Lord of everything that lives: Lord, have mercy.
We confess you as Head of your body, the Church: Christ . . .
We acclaim you as the One who fills all creation: Lord . . .

OPENING PRAYER:

Rejoicing in Christ our hope, let us pray that he may send the Holy Spirit into our hearts as the pledge of his continuing presence in our midst.

READINGS:

1) **Acts 1:1-11.** Taken from the book of Acts, our first reading assures us that the same Jesus who died and rose will come again.

2) **Eph. 1:17-23.** Writing to the Church at Ephesus, Paul tells Christians they are called to a hope that will bring them to a full knowledge of God's plan for their holiness.

3) **Mk. 16:15-20.** The faith community of the baptized is charged to continue Christ's mission of preaching, healing, and consoling.

HOMILY NOTES:

● Christ's life was a journey back to his Father, taking the whole of mankind with him. The Ascension was not a space flight, but a sign that Christ had returned to his Father, had left the earth with its limits of time and space, and is now reigning with the Father.

● As baptized Christians we are part of his Body, which is now glorified in heaven. So our glorification has begun. Hope is not wishful thinking. Hope means living in the certainty of resurrection and new life in Christ. Hope is not optimism either.

● Here we suffer tension between our spirits already sharing in Christ's new life through Baptism and our bodies still subject to death. But our journey, however difficult, will take us back to the Father if we follow Christ.

● People are searching for some sureness in their lives. We Christians have it. At the Ascension, Christ bade us go and share with others.

GENERAL INTERCESSIONS:

Invitation: Hope is a creative force that can revolutionize human lives through the promise of a better future. Since we have been called to live by hope, let us offer our petitions to the Father, who never disappoints those who trust in him. Our response is: **LORD, WE HOPE IN YOU.**

1. That the Church may boldly proclaim Christ's message of hope in a world which seeks a better, more peaceful future, we pray to the Lord.

2. That as a new people reborn through water and the Holy Spirit, we may approach the complexities of modern life with joyful confidence, we . . .

3. That as members of Christ's body we may have a deep reverence for the sacredness of all human life, we . . .

4. For all those whose lives are without hope and without faith, we . . .

5. For persons who feel they have nothing to live for, that our love for them may renew their spirit of hope, we . . .

*(Additional invocations)*_____

Conclusion: Father, through Christ you have called us to be signs of hope for those who live in darkness and despair. Inspire us to carry on the work of your Son, even when weakness and doubt threaten to undermine our efforts. We make our prayer through Christ our Lord.

ADDITIONAL INVITATION TO COMMUNION:
Behold the Christ who is the hope of all creation!

PRAYER AFTER COMMUNION:
"May Christ enlighten the eyes of your mind, so that you can see what hope his call holds for you." Let us rededicate ourselves to the task of offering hope to persons who feel that life is futile and without meaning.

Seventh Sunday of Easter

THEME: CO-WORKERS WITH CHRIST

INTRODUCTION:
In its document on the Church in the modern world, Vatican II remarked that the joys and hopes, the griefs and anxieties of this age are fully shared by Christians. As co-workers with Christ, we are a people sent to announce God's truth in the world. Sometimes this will mean taking critical and unpopular stands against elements in modern life which are contrary to the Gospel. But Christ has prayed that the Father may send his Spirit to strengthen us.

INVITATION TO PENITENTIAL RITE:
Jesus has prayed that we may be consecrated in truth and sent into the world. Let us consider the times we have been more interested in seeking personal comfort than in searching for ways to present Christ's truth to men of our day.

FORM C: *(Optional invocations)*
Your passion was the way to resurrection and life: Lord, have mercy.
Your prayer was that we might witness to the truth: Christ . . .
Your promise was to send the Spirit upon those who believe in you:
   Lord . . .

OPENING PRAYER:
Following the example of Jesus, who prayed for us on the night before he suffered, let us ask that all men may be one in the Father's love.

READINGS:
1) **Acts 1:15-17, 20-26.** The ministry of the apostles was crucial for the early Church. In this selection from Acts, we hear how the apostles prayed and then elected Matthias to replace Judas in the apostolic ministry.

2) **1 Jn. 4:11-16.** The reason why we can love others is because God has first loved us so much. We testify to this love as co-workers with Christ.

3) **Jn. 17:11-19.** Jesus prays, knowing that his disciples will encounter opposition and even hatred in the world.

HOMILY NOTES:
● At the Last Supper Jesus prayed for his disciples and all those who believe through the words of the apostles; ourselves, that is, and those we bring to the knowledge and love of Christ.

● Jesus knew that, unaided, we would be unequal to our task, be hated by the world, and be exposed to evil. We do not belong to the world, the world of the materialist, any more than Christ does.

● But he has sent us to the world of God's good creation and the men in it. By our labor and technical skill the earth is made more fruitful, and by our example and word, men are brought to acknowledge the rule of Christ.

GENERAL INTERCESSIONS:

Invitation: We sometimes forget that Jesus prayed not only for his apostles, but also for those who would come to believe in him through the apostles' preaching. Since we know Christ lives in us through his Spirit, let us unite in prayer, as we respond: **LORD, FILL OUR HEARTS.**

1. That as co-workers with Christ we may accept our responsibility to make the Father's truth and love known in the world, we pray to the Lord.

2. That we may be courageous in criticizing those elements of modern life which threaten the dignity and destiny of human beings, we . . .

3. That Jesus' prayer for the unity of all who believe in him may soon be fulfilled, we . . .

4. For persons driven from their homes by the catastrophe of war, we . . .

5. For families torn apart by tension and disagreement, we . . .

*(Additional invocations)*_____

Conclusion: We offer you these petitions, Father, in union with the prayer of your Son. Fill our hearts with the joy that comes from knowing you; renew in us the Spirit of truth, and give us sturdy hands to do your work and confident hearts to praise your name, through Christ our Lord.

ADDITIONAL INVITATION TO COMMUNION:
Behold the Lord who shares his Spirit with us!

PRAYER AFTER COMMUNION:
These words of Christ were heard today in John's Gospel: "Consecrate them in the truth . . . I have sent them into the world." Refreshed by our reception of the risen Lord, let us ask for fidelity in our mission as co-workers with Christ for the life of the world.

Pentecost

THEME: THE COMING OF THE SPIRIT

INTRODUCTION:

The term used for God's Spirit in the Old Testament literally means "breath." When God's Spirit came upon a person, it meant that the very life-breath of God moved within him. Similarly the Gospels picture the risen Jesus breathing on the disciples to give them his Spirit, his new life. Filled with the same Spirit of Jesus through Baptism, we have the privilege of living with the very life-breath of God.

INVITATION TO PENITENTIAL RITE:

My brothers and sisters, the Spirit which we have received is one of peace and forgiveness. Let us remember that we will be forgiven in the measure in which we are willing to pardon the faults of others.

FORM C: *(Optional invocations)*

Your creating Spirit gives life and breath to the work of your hands: Lord, have mercy.

Your consoling Spirit is a Father for the poor and dejected: Christ . . .

Your forgiving Spirit replaces our sinfulness with your love: Lord . . .

OPENING PRAYER:

Several times in the Acts of the Apostles, the Spirit is described as coming when Christians were gathered for prayer. Let us ask that he come to us now, to open our hearts to the meaning of the Scriptures.

READINGS:

1) **Acts 2:1-11.** One of Luke's favorite themes is that salvation is universal, intended for everyone. We hear that theme reflected in today's reading from Acts, which describes the Spirit's dramatic coming and the apostles' bold preaching of God's wonderful works.

2) **1 Cor. 12:3-7, 12-13.** Paul writes that the influence of the Spirit is felt in every aspect of Christian life: in our profession of faith, in our gifts of mutual service, in our worship.

3) **Jn. 20:19-23.** The peace of Christ takes full effect in the life of believers when they receive the Spirit who forgives sin.

HOMILY NOTES:

● We think with envy of those who walked with Christ in the flesh. But we have the Spirit of Jesus, not a poor substitute, but his own life, living in us.

● We share Christ's roles: as priest, as prophet, and as king. As priest, together offering Christ to his Father in the Mass; as prophet, preaching Christ by our words and actions; as king, building up the community into the Kingdom of God.

● How can we make best use of all that the Spirit of Christ is offering? He works through our intelligence, giving deeper insights into his truth (but we must do our part, too); through our will, to strengthening our resolve to live as sons of God in everyday difficulties; through our work, making our poor efforts to build the Kingdom fruitful in his way.

● The Spirit blows where it wills; but principally through his Church, of which we are members. The Spirit will fill us with the love of God. We must show in our actions that we are moved by the Spirit to love others with the love that Christ has shown.

GENERAL INTERCESSIONS:

Invitation: St. Paul once said that, when we do not know what we should pray for, the Spirit prays in us and for us. Although we may feel weak and inept at prayer, let us call upon the Father with the confident assurance of children, as we respond: **SEND US YOUR SPIRIT, LORD.**

1. That the Holy Spirit may breathe new life into the Church and cause it to grow in unity and holiness, we pray to the Lord.

2. That the Spirit of truth may inspire those who hold public office with honesty and foresight in governing the destiny of men and nations, we . . .

3. That the Spirit of consolation may wipe away the tears of persons who are overcome by sadness, we . . .

4. That the creating Spirit may assist those who work to improve the quality of human life through medicine and science, we . . .

5. That the Spirit of the Lord may fill the young with a hopeful vision of the future, and the old with the wisdom of experience, we . . .

*(Additional invocations)*_____

Conclusion: Send us your Spirit, Father, so that we may live and breathe with your own life. Aided by your consolation, may we work for the growth of your Kingdom in the hearts of men, through Christ our Lord.

ADDITIONAL INVITATION TO COMMUNION:

Behold the Lord who breathes the Spirit of forgiveness into our hearts.

PRAYER AFTER COMMUNION:

"The disciples were filled with joy when they saw the Lord . . . And he breathed on them and said, 'Receive the Holy Spirit.' " In the Spirit we have offered this Eucharist as God's priestly people. Let us pray now that the same Spirit may re-create the world in justice and truth.

Trinity Sunday
Sunday after Pentecost

THEME: THE PRESENCE OF GOD

INTRODUCTION:

God is not a riddle to be solved, but a life to be lived. Men know God only through a life of faith lived in communion with other believers: Israel heard God speaking from the heart of the fire; Paul saw him in everyone led by the Spirit; Jesus knew him as the Father with whom he was one. We, too, experience God's presence in the Scriptures, in worship, in creation, and in the sacrament of our brother.

INVITATION TO PENITENTIAL RITE:

The Holy Spirit bears witness that we are sons of God and brothers of Jesus. If our actions recently have not conformed to God's personal presence in us, let us take this opportunity to be sorry.

FORM C: *(Optional invocations)*

Word of the Father, through whom all things were created: Lord, have mercy.

Brother of men, sharing our weakness: Christ . . .

Lord of the Church, giver of the Spirit: Lord . . .

OPENING PRAYER:

As a community made one with the very unity of Father, Son, and Spirit, let us pray for a moment in silence.

READINGS:

1) **Dt. 4:32-34, 39-40.** One of the major ideas in the Book of Deuteronomy is God's active presence to his people. In the passage we hear today, Moses recalls the signs and wonders by which God made Israel a holy and chosen nation.

2) **Rom. 8:14-17.** Paul picks up the theme of God's presence to men by stressing our participation in the Spirit who prompts us to call God "Father" and makes us co-heirs with Jesus.

3) **Mt. 28:16-20.** As the apostles go forth to preach and baptize, Jesus promises to be forever present with them and with all who believe their message.

HOMILY NOTES:

● Today's exploration of space has shown us something of the greatness of the God who created the universe. We can appreciate it more than people in past centuries. All the same, in whatever century we may live, it is totally beyond us to comprehend God.

● He knows how limited we are and he has sent his Son to show us what God is like. "He who sees me, sees the Father," said Jesus. As man, Jesus, like ourselves, was limited by time and space. He could only meet and know the people around him during his life in Palestine. But he has given us his Spirit, and now all men can know him.

● We received his Spirit at Baptism, when we accepted a part in Jesus' life, death, and resurrection. Sharing, therefore, in Jesus' life, we share his work of making the Father known to men. With the Spirit in us to help us, we accept this mission.

GENERAL INTERCESSIONS:

Invitation: Our union as God's children in truth and charity reveals the unity of God's own personal life. Today, as in the past, God lives in the midst of human beings: Jesus and the Father are one with anyone who believes, and the Spirit is present as counselor and guide. With joy, then, let us pray: **STAY WITH US, LORD.**

1. That the Church may continue to reveal God's presence among men through its solid faith and its active charity, we pray to the Lord.

2. That God's Kingdom, revealed in the person of Jesus, may come into the hearts of men who seek a deeper significance for human life, we . . .

3. That the union of married Christians may reflect ever more clearly the tender love Christ has for his Church, we . . .

4. That persons for whom poverty and oppression have made God seem absent may find in us a sacrament of his presence, we . . .

*(Additional invocations)*_____

Conclusion: We rejoice in your presence, Father, because you are a lover of mankind. Gather us together in the Spirit and make us truly your Church, a people bought with the precious blood of Jesus your Son. We make our prayer through the same Christ our Lord.

ADDITIONAL INVITATION TO COMMUNION:
Behold Jesus, Son of the Father and Giver of the Spirit!

PRAYER AFTER COMMUNION:
"Go . . . make disciples of all nations . . . baptize them in the name of the Father and of the Son and of the Holy Spirit." Let us pray that the faith which makes us missionaries may grow as a result of the unity we have shared at the Lord's table.

Corpus Christi

THEME: THE BOND BETWEEN GOD AND MAN

INTRODUCTION:
For the people of the Old Testament blood meant life itself. The blood of Temple sacrifices and the blood used in ceremonies of covenant renewal meant the people were bonded to God in a communion of life. On the night before he died, Jesus told us that the Eucharistic cup we share would be his own blood, the blood of a new covenant between God and men. Through the blood of Christ we are reconciled to God, made brothers of one another, and made privileged to live God's own life.

INVITATION TO PENITENTIAL RITE:
The blood of Jesus, we are told in the second reading, has purified us from dead actions so we can serve the living God. Let us ask pardon for the moments when we have served our own gods — gods of prejudice or profit — rather than the living Father of Christ.

FORM C: *(Optional invocations)*
Your blood has reconciled us with the Father: Lord, have mercy.
Your blood has cancelled our sins and restored us to life: Christ . . .
Your blood has made us a people ready to serve the Father: Lord . . .

OPENING PRAYER:
Because we are a community of brothers and sisters redeemed by Christ's blood, let us pray for a deeper bond of faith and love with God.

READINGS:
1) **Ex. 24:3-8.** The covenant, a permanent bond between God and Israel, is central to the book of Exodus. In this passage we hear how Moses cast the blood of sacrifice on the people and thereby sealed their communion with the God who delivered them from Egypt.

2) **Heb. 9:11-15.** The author of the Letter to the Hebrews contrasts the repeated Temple sacrifices with what Jesus accomplished. The blood of Christ cancels our sins once and for all.

3) **Mk. 14:12-16, 22-26.** A new bond is created between God and man through the blood of Jesus, which is "poured out for many."

HOMILY NOTES:
● On Mount Sinai, God entered into a relationship with the people of Israel. He would be their God; they would be his people and keep his commandments. Moses acted as mediator between God and the people.

- Animals were sacrificed and offered to God. Animal blood was taken; and some was given to God by pouring it on the altar, and some was given to the people by its being cast toward them. God and men were in communion. This ceremony was only a temporary substitute for the reality to come.

- On Calvary God entered into a new and lasting relationship with his people — us. He is our God, we his people. This time it was the God-Man, Jesus, who acted as mediator. Christ offered a perfect sacrifice to his Father — himself. By pouring out his life's blood, he united us with God. His blood sealed the relationship forever.

GENERAL INTERCESSIONS:

Invitation: Although our individual relationship with God is vitally important, the community Eucharist emphasizes our *common* bond with the Father through the blood of our brother Jesus. Let us strive to be truly one in heart and mind, as we pray: **LORD, UNITE US IN LOVE.**

1. That the Church may always seek its source of renewal at the table of God's Word and the table of Christ's body and blood, we pray to the Lord.

2. That this and every Eucharist may contribute to our common growth in the bond of charity and peace, we . . .

3. That our faith in Christ's presence in the Eucharist may be matched by our faith in his presence among the poor, the sick, and the lonely, we . . .

4. For those who are prevented from discovering the Bread of Life because they lack the ordinary bread of physical nourishment, we . . .

5. For the men and women who help us plan and prepare our parish Eucharistic celebrations, we . . .

*(Additional invocations)*_____

Conclusion: Father, as you transform our gifts of bread and wine through the action of your Spirit, transform also our lives and our world. Help us become what we receive — the body of Christ broken in mercy for the salvation of all men. We make our prayer through the same Christ our Lord.

ADDITIONAL INVITATION TO COMMUNION:

Behold the body and blood of the new and everlasting covenant!

PRAYER AFTER COMMUNION:

"This is my blood, the blood of the covenant, which is to be poured out for many." Since we are the people of a new covenant, let us pray, pledging ourselves to bring Christ's transforming presence into our homes and our work.

Sacred Heart
Third Friday after Pentecost

THEME: GOD'S PERSISTENT LOVE

INTRODUCTION:
Unlike a lot of human efforts, God's love doesn't quit. It seeks man, pursues him, and never gets tired of offering new opportunities for discovery. The dying and rising of Jesus reveal most clearly the lengths to which God's persistent love will go. If, then, we let Christ live in our hearts by faith, we will be rooted in love and filled with the utter fullness of God himself.

INVITATION TO PENITENTIAL RITE:
God is the Holy One who wants to heal men, not destroy them. Let us recall the ways we have rejected God's offer of healing by refusing to admit our weakness and our need for help.

FORM C: *(Optional invocations)*
When we were no people at all, your love made us God's People: Lord, have mercy.

When we were weak and without hope, your love gave us the power to grow strong: Christ . . .

When we were frightened and insecure, your love rooted us in confident faith: Lord . . .

OPENING PRAYER:
Let us pray for some understanding of the breadth and length, the height and depth of God's love revealed in the heart of Jesus.

READINGS:
1) **Hos. 11:1, 3-4, 8-9.** Our first reading from the prophet Hosea reveals a God whose love for his wayward people is as tender as that of a father for a little child just learning to walk.

2) **Eph. 3:8-12, 14-19.** Paul writes that from all eternity God's plan was to show men the depth of his love in Jesus Christ.

3) **Jn. 19:31-37.** As he slept in death on the cross, Jesus' side poured forth blood and water, the signs of his intense love.

HOMILY NOTES:
● God pursues his people Israel; he is like a hunter going in search of his prey. But he pursues in order to heal and not to hurt. Israel did not understand this, for God says, "The more I called to them the more they went from me." The Old Testament is a continuous story of God refusing to give up the chase in spite of Israel's adultery.

- What more could God do? He comes as man. His concern is always for the faithless and helpless sinners, the handicapped, the unloved. His concern is total, and such totality can be shown only in a death.

- His passion and death can only be understood if seen as an act of love. Christ's love is for man as he is; that is, full of failings.

- In the Mass, Christ's act of love is made present. Only sinners can feel at home here. This is a feast of confidence and trust in God's love for us.

GENERAL INTERCESSIONS:

Invitation: We heard St. Paul say we should be bold enough to approach God in complete confidence. Relying on the boundless love of our Father, let us place before him our deepest cares and concerns, as we pray: **IN YOUR LOVE, LORD, HEAR US.**

1. That God's persistent love may fill his Church with tireless energy to work for a just peace among men, we pray to the Lord.

2. That the Father of the poor may bless the efforts of those who labor for a more reasonable distribution of wealth and material goods, we . . .

3. That the members of this parish may grow in the love of Christ which surpasses all understanding, we . . .

4. For people whose lives have been hardened and embittered by years of injustice and misery, we . . .

5. For those intentions which are in our hearts, but which we do not know how to express in words, we . . .

*(Additional invocations)*_____

Conclusion: Father, the height and depth of your love for men were revealed in the heart of Jesus, your Son. Grant us, through the power of your Spirit, to grow strong in faith, more lively in charity, and more generous in service to your Church and your world. We make our prayer through Christ our Lord.

ADDITIONAL INVITATION TO COMMUNION:

Behold him who loved us even to the point of death!

PRAYER AFTER COMMUNION:

"May Christ dwell in your hearts through faith," that your life may be rooted in love. Let us pray for a love that is closer to that of Jesus in the Gospels — one that seeks to include the unlovable and even our enemies.

71

Second Sunday of the Year

THEME: GOD'S CALL

INTRODUCTION:

Ours is an age of remarkable progress in communications media. Radio, telephone, and television allow almost instant contact with anyone and any place. Even our language reflects this; we speak of "giving someone a call" when we want to contact him by phone. God also communicates with men by means of a call, a call that comes through a variety of channels. He beckons men to himself through the Gospel, through creation itself, through the worshipping community. Let us open our hearts to that call, wherever and however it may come to us.

INVITATION TO PENITENTIAL RITE:

Despite the varied means of communication at our disposal, we often fail to hear either God or our neighbor calling us. Let us remind ourselves of ways we have failed to listen attentively to the Word of God or to the words of others who needed us.

FORM C: *(Optional invocations)*

Through the prophets you spoke of the promise of salvation: Lord, have mercy.

Through the Gospel you called us to faith and conversion of heart: Christ . . .

Through the Spirit you continue to call us together as a people: Lord . . .

OPENING PRAYER:

Let us pray, opening our hearts and minds to God's call in the Scriptures we are about to hear.

READINGS:

1) **1 Sm. 3:3-10, 19.** The first reading of today's liturgy provides a classic example of God's call and man's response. The boy Samuel is ready to listen to whatever God may want to tell him.

2) **1 Cor. 6:13-15, 17-20.** Paul tells us that the Christian cannot withold any aspect of his life from God's call to holiness. Because he is a temple of the Spirit, the Christian's dedication to God must be total, including heart, mind, body, emotions, personality.

3) **Jn. 1:35-42.** As the Father called Jesus to be his Servant, so disciples must be willing to follow the call of Jesus — wherever it may lead them.

HOMILY NOTES:

• At Baptism, our lips and ears are anointed so that we can hear the call of Christ, and go and tell others about him. We must always be ready to say to God, like Samuel, "Speak, Lord; your servant is listening."

● The voice of Christ comes to us in Scripture, in the faith of the apostles which we have been given, and in the cries for help, spoken and unspoken, of our fellowmen. Willingness to listen implies a willingness to follow, like the two disciples.

● We may at times want to avoid the call of Christ; it disturbs our comfort and complacency. Jesus suffered for us and all men; so "we are not our own property." We must give ourselves to a God who has already given himself to us if we are to realize the purpose of our existence, our vocation.

● We have to be the people God wants us to be, and do the job he intended for us.

GENERAL INTERCESSIONS:

Invitation: Whenever we pray together we do so as members of the one body of Christ and as living temples of the Spirit. Since we are confident that such prayer, made in the name of Jesus, will always be heard, let us respond: **IN YOUR NAME WE PRAY, LORD.**

1. That the Church may effectively use the modern means of social communication to proclaim the Gospel to the ends of the earth, we pray to the Lord.

2. That those who have the responsibility of reporting and interpreting news in the public media may be guided by principles of justice, charity, and truth, we . . .

3. That we may hear Christ's call in the voices of the poor, the sick, and the aged who cry out for help, we . . .

4. That we may encourage those whom God calls to service in the ministry and in religious communities, we . . .

5. For our young people who have committed themselves to work among the economically deprived and socially disadvantaged, we . . .

*(Additional invocations)*_____

Conclusion: We call upon you, Father, in the name of Jesus, confident that you will hear us. Like Samuel, the prophet of old, we listen for your voice and ask for an enthusiastic readiness to do your will in all things, through Christ our Lord.

ADDITIONAL INVITATION TO COMMUNION:
Behold Christ, with whom we are one body in the Spirit!

PRAYER AFTER COMMUNION:
"You know, surely, that your bodies are members making up the body of Christ." Let us pray, remembering that, as we are one body and one Spirit in Christ, we are responsible for the lives of one another.

Third Sunday of the Year

THEME: OUR RESPONSE TO GOD

INTRODUCTION:

Historians are fond of pointing out how civilizations arise, grow powerful, and then disappear. You don't have to be an historian to realize that the world we live in, with its space flights and atomic power plants, is radically different from what our great-grandparents knew. Yet, for all its rapid change and development, this world is still God's world. He still loves it, but he leaves us free either to respond to his love or to make a shambles of his creation.

INVITATION TO PENITENTIAL RITE:

Our freedom can be a frightening responsibility; at every turn it confronts us with a choice between happiness or misery, life or death. Let us reflect on the times we have abused our freedom by refusing to make responsible choices about our lives and our work.

FORM C: *(Optional invocations)*

You taught us how to live without fear, and love without limit: Lord, have mercy.

You challenged us to use our freedom constructively and creatively: Christ . . .

You called us to believe and to repent of our former way of life: Lord . . .

OPENING PRAYER:

Since God has called us to faith in the Gospel, let us respond by praying for the full coming of his Kingdom among men.

READINGS:

1) **Jon. 3:1-5, 10.** The story of Jonah has two important points: it reveals the universal nature of God's mercy, and it shows the effects of true repentance. If we answer God's call to renounce evil, his mercy will overshadow our lives, bringing them peace.

2) **1 Cor. 7:29-31.** For a time Paul seems to have thought that the end of the world was near. Although he changed this opinion later, his message is still vital: Christians should live totally for God.

3) **Mk. 1:14-20.** Jesus announces that the Kingdom of God is breaking in upon the world. Our response to his message must be faith and repentance.

HOMILY NOTES:

● God called Jonah to tell the people of Nineveh to turn to him again. Jonah found that this request went against the grain, but after a struggle he did go to the people of Nineveh and they turned back to God.

74

- We are sometimes called to do difficult things to help make the Father known. If we attempt them, he will do the rest.

- Peter, Andrew, James and John were called by Christ to leave all and follow him. Their response was immediate. They were unlikely people — simple, uneducated fishermen — to tell the Good News to a sophisticated world empire. Yet because they responded, by the strength of the Holy Spirit they were responsible for continuing Christ's work.

- If we are to be useful in continuing Christ's work, it means responding to the call not just once but day after day. It means caring for others, getting involved, showing God's love in our lives. It is what we are, and what we do, knowing that God is all powerful, that will make God's call real to us and all those who share our lives.

GENERAL INTERCESSIONS:

Invitation: Prayer is the moment when we can exercise our freedom to the utmost by choosing to unmask and unburden ourselves in the presence of the Father who judges and saves. In a spirit of freedom, let us respond: **LORD, WE TRUST IN YOUR MERCY.**

1. That the hearts of all men may be converted to the Lord, who calls the world to repentance, we pray to the Lord.

2. That we may accept the full message of the Gospel, including those hard sayings that speak of trouble and the Cross, we . . .

3. That the Holy Spirit may inspire courageous, decisive leadership in the Church, we . . .

4. That we may work with Christ as fishers of men, drawing the world closer to the Kingdom that is near at hand, we . . .

5. For persons afflicted with nervous disorders and for those who are in mental hospitals, we . . .

*(Additional invocations)*_____

Conclusion: Father, give us the wisdom to live totally for you. When our courage fails, support us; when our hope begins to fade, renew us; when our charity grows cold, rekindle it. Make us the heralds of your Good News to a world that needs the reassurance of your love, through Christ our Lord.

ADDITIONAL INVITATION TO COMMUNION:
Behold the Lord whose kingdom is near at hand!

PRAYER AFTER COMMUNION:
"The kingdom of God is close at hand; repent and believe the Good News." Let us respond to Christ's gift of himself in this Eucharist by giving ourselves to prayer and work for the full coming of his Kingdom in us and in the world.

Fourth Sunday of the Year

THEME: AUTHORITY

INTRODUCTION:

It has been said that one of the great crises of our time is the problem of authority in homes, civil society, and the Church. If we turn to the Gospels for help in facing this problem, we will discover that Jesus was a man of authority not because he ruled people, but because he was able to call forth the best in each man. Like every genuine prophet, Jesus knew how to read the signs of the times and, though he lived as a servant, his teaching had the authority of love and truth behind it.

INVITATION TO PENITENTIAL RITE:

Jesus' authority flowed from a heart altogether responsive to the Father's word and will. Let us recall how we have exercised authority in our homes and at work: were we high-handed and bossy, or did we follow Christ's pattern of humble service?

FORM C: *(Optional invocations)*

As servant of men, you were meek and humble of heart: Lord, have mercy.

As prophet of the Kingdom, you spoke the word of the Father in truth: Christ . . .

As the Holy One of God, you taught the way of salvation: Lord . . .

OPENING PRAYER:

Let us pray that we may become prophets who know both how to listen in silence and when to speak in God's name.

READINGS:

1) **Dt. 18:15-20.** Every age has had its true and false prophets. Our first reading from the book of Deuteronomy, gives us a way to tell the difference: the true prophet speaks only the words God has given him.

2) **1 Cor. 7:32-35.** Every Christian is called to devote his best energies and talents to the service of Christ and his brothers. Paul suggests that some may do this more easily by remaining unmarried.

3) **Mk. 1:21-28.** Mark is especially interested in showing the manner and effects of Christ's teaching. Jesus speaks "with authority," that is, with the full power of God at work in him.

HOMILY NOTES:

● The authority of Christ is innate. He has the freedom to act by virtue of his possession of truth, because he was sent by the Father. Hence he has competence also.

• Authority is not the same as jurisdiction — power over others. Authority expresses the confident freedom of those filled with Christ's Spirit to act and teach. Yet it may not be used to stifle the Spirit in others (Thes. 5:18). The word of God is not bound. There are varieties of gifts but the same Spirit.

• Christ said, "Whoever would be great among you must be your servant." His own authority was expressed in service. Our authority must be modelled on his. A doctor exercises authority by virtue of his skill and experience, but expresses it in service to his patient. We remember that Christ often acted as a healer, but never as a ruler.

GENERAL INTERCESSIONS:

Invitation: A person with real authority doesn't have to browbeat people to show that he has it; if his authority is genuine, people will recognize it as coming from God's own power, truth, and love. This is the kind of authority found in Jesus — one based on humility, open dialogue, and readiness to forget and forgive. Let us pray that God will bless his Church with such authority, as we respond: **LORD, BLESS YOUR PEOPLE.**

1. That authority in the Church may always be expressed as the humble service of brothers bound together by a common Spirit of truth, we pray to the Lord.

2. That government officials may pattern their exercise of authority on the model of Jesus, who came to serve rather than be served, we . . .

3. That parents may, by their authority in the home, seek more to love and be loved than to create an atmosphere of repression and fear, we . . .

4. That we may respect authority, but not fear to criticize its abuses, we . . .

*(Additional invocations)*_____

Conclusion: We know, Father, that real authority is an expression of your concern for our well-being. In an age when everyone seems to be talking, help us listen in order to discern the true from the false, the genuine from the phony. Give us hearts that seek your word and will in all things and above all things, through Christ our Lord.

ADDITIONAL INVITATION TO COMMUNION:
Behold Christ, the prophet who speaks only the words of God!

PRAYER AFTER COMMUNION:
Mark told us that Jesus' teaching "made a deep impression . . . because he taught with authority." Filled with the Spirit through this Eucharist, let us pray for the wisdom to hear God speaking through men of our own time and place.

Fifth Sunday of the Year

THEME: FREEDOM

INTRODUCTION:

Today we are keenly aware of the factors that can inhibit human freedom. And we rightly oppose those forms of physical and psychological pressure which make slaves out of human beings. The Gospels show that Jesus' purpose was to free man from everything that stands in the way of genuine freedom: sickness, malice, even death itself.

INVITATION TO PENITENTIAL RITE:

Paul claims, in today's second reading, that he never insisted on the rights he had as a preacher of the Gospel. Perhaps we have sometimes insisted so much on having our own way that we have crushed the rights of other people. If we have, let us take this moment to be sorry.

FORM C: *(Optional invocations)*

By taking on our weakness, you freed us from sin and death: Lord, have mercy.

By healing our sickness, you freed us for service to others: Christ...

By seeking our love, you freed us from slavery to selfishness: Lord...

OPENING PRAYER:

Uniting ourselves with Christ, who sought quiet and solitude for prayer, let us pray for a few moments in silence.

READINGS:

1) **Jb. 7:1-4, 6-7.** Job has usually been depicted as a model of patience in adversity. But this picture is not wholly accurate: Job complained bitterly about the tragedies of his life, and today we hear him in a very pessimistic mood, moaning about life's apparent emptiness.

2) **1 Cor. 9:16-19, 22-23.** Paul felt the urgency of proclaiming the Gospel to every man. He did this by opening himself to share the weakness, the sorrow and the joy of others as though they were his own.

3) **Mk. 1:29-39.** Jesus continues his work as a liberator by freeing Simon's mother from illness and freeing possessed persons from the power of evil.

HOMILY NOTES:

● Without Christ, our life on earth seems wearisome, hard and dull, empty of meaning, ending in death. We must become servants of

Christ if we want to live life to the full. If we serve Christ, we become truly free.

● But to serve Christ means that we must make ourselves the servants of everyone we meet. To do so will not be easy. People will demand more and more of us. They will want our time, our sympathy, our practical help in all problems that each day brings.

● If we refuse to listen to them, then we ourselves are the ones to suffer. We are condemning ourselves to real slavery to our own selfishness, ending in death. But if we gladly serve our neighbor, imitating Christ in his service to the sick and helpless, then we are serving Christ, too. And by doing so we gain freedom here and now. God will no longer call us his servants; we shall become his friends.

GENERAL INTERCESSIONS:

Invitation: Christ liberated us from the destructive powers of evil and sin so that we could be free to cooperate with him in spreading the Good News. Since we cannot do this work without his help, let us pray: **LORD, BE OUR FREEDOM.**

1. That the Church may seek to free persons from whatever stands in the way of communicating the Gospel to men of our times, we pray to the Lord.

2. That men who cry out against the injustices which enslave human beings may be supported by all of us in the Church, we . . .

3. That following the example of Paul, we may preach the Good News freely, without seeking financial profit from it, we . . .

4. That we may work for the salvation of all by sharing their weaknesses, joys, and sorrows, we . . .

5. For men and women who have given up comfort and security in order to work among the sick and the destitute, we . . .

*(Additional invocations)*_____

Conclusion: Free us, Father, from whatever enslaves us to lives of comfortable mediocrity. Enable us to be bold in our prayer and work for the Gospel, so that we may free others for happiness in your service, through Christ our Lord.

ADDITIONAL INVITATION TO COMMUNION:

Behold Christ, our Freedom and our Life!

PRAYER AFTER COMMUNION:

Paul told us today that his joy consisted in being "able to offer the Good News free." Let us pray that the joy we have experienced at this holy table may cause us to offer our time and concern freely to others for the sake of the Gospel.

Sixth Sunday of the Year

THEME: MAN RESTORED

INTRODUCTION:

During the paschal vigil the Church sings the jubilant Easter Proclamation *(Exsultet)*. In that beautiful hymn it is said that Christ's resurrection restores the whole world to grace and peace, that all of creation is rescued from darkness and restored to light and life. Through Christ, God can take even the most miserable human situation and transform it into an occasion for celebrating. This is not because God is a magician, but because he knows how to *love* dead men back to life, sick men back to health, and sinful men back to peace.

INVITATION TO PENITENTIAL RITE:

We need to remind ourselves regularly that, as Christians, we are called to live for others. Let us seek God's ready mercy for the times we have taken unfair advantage of others instead of working for their salvation.

FORM C: *(Optional invocations)*

Your Gospel restores peace to the weak and sinful: Lord, have mercy.

Your power to heal restores hope to the sick: Christ . . .

Your rising from death restores grace to all the world: Lord . . .

OPENING PRAYER:

Taking Christ as our model, let us pray that the world may be restored to unity and peace.

READINGS:

1) **Lv. 13:1-2, 44-46.** Leprosy was the disease most dreaded by the ancient Jew because it cut him off from the community and religious life of Israel. Our selection from Leviticus describes the ritual prescribed for one suffering from such a disease.

2) **1 Cor. 10:31—11:1.** Paul asks that whatever Christians do should be done for God's glory and the building up of the faith community.

3) **Mk. 1:40-45.** Mark describes how even the dreadful disease of leprosy yields to Jesus' power. We also get an insight into the very human compassion of the Lord for those who are suffering.

HOMILY NOTES:

● Our world knows many outcasts, the down-and-out, the alcoholic, the neurotic, the lonely, and all the unwanted. We avoid them. Our society excludes those whose culture or way of life is different. Even we, the Church, tend to be exclusive.

● Jesus cleansed the leper and restored him to his world; then the man could enjoy life again, work, company, family, and friends. Jesus set up God's Kingdom. In that Kingdom we are all sinners who have been restored to God's favor.

● Sinful man without Christ can no more belong to the Kingdom than a leper could belong to the town community. But once healed, he truly belongs; no one is an outcast from Christ's Kingdom, which is here now. We are members on one claim alone, that of men restored to friendship with God through his mercy.

GENERAL INTERCESSIONS:

Invitation: Compassion was one of the most attractive qualities of Jesus' personality. His tender reaction to the leper of today's Gospel reveals a deep sensitivity to the suffering and embarrassment of other persons. Let us pray for similar compassion and understanding, as we respond: **LORD, CURE US.**

1. That the sick and dying may be strengthened in mind and body by our prayer and the Church's sacrament of anointing, we pray to the Lord.

2. That those whom poverty and mental anguish have made social lepers may be helped by our compassion and work for them, we . . .

3. That doctors and scientists may be aided in their work for the elimination of incurable diseases, we . . .

4. That more Christians may accept the call to provide homes for orphans and unwanted children, we . . .

5. For a deeper understanding of the differences which divide parents and children, we . . .

*(Additional invocations)*_____

Conclusion: Merciful Father, deepen our spirit of compassion and understanding for those who suffer. We want to model our lives on the pattern of Jesus, who never sought his own advantage, but rather sought freedom, healing and peace for every man. We make our prayer through the same Christ our Lord.

ADDITIONAL INVITATION TO COMMUNION:

Behold the Lord who restores freedom and peace to all creation!

PRAYER AFTER COMMUNION:

To the leper who sought a cure in today's Gospel, Jesus stretched out his hand, touched him and said: "Be cured!" As we have been touched by Christ's healing presence in this sacrament, let us pray, reaching out to embrace the world in compassionate love.

Seventh Sunday of the Year

THEME: WHOLENESS

INTRODUCTION:

Despite spectacular progress in science and technology, man often is plagued by a sense of incompleteness. There is something unfinished about man — something that gnaws at him, that unsettles and disturbs his deepest roots. Christ came to complete man, to make him whole, to render him fully alive and conscious of his mission and destiny as a lord of creation and a son of God. This work of completion and wholeness is still going on; but we are confident of final success because, in Jesus Christ, God said "Yes" to man once and for all.

INVITATION TO PENITENTIAL RITE:

Sometimes we are so burdened by past failings that we are afraid to look with confidence toward the future. Let us stop for a moment to remember that our Father's mercy is new every day, that he is ready to forgive even before we think of asking.

FORM C: *(Optional invocations)*

You are God's "Yes" to a world longing for redemption: Lord, have mercy.

You make broken men whole again by forgiving their sins: Christ . . .

You draw all creation toward fulfillment by the action and presence of your Spirit: Lord . . .

OPENING PRAYER:

Let us offer prayer to the Father who has said "Yes" to all his promises through Christ our Savior.

READINGS:

1) **Is. 43:18-19, 21-22, 24-25.** Exile was a terrible shock to Israel's conviction that it was a chosen, holy people. But through the prophet Isaiah God promises he will forget Israel's past failures and form a new people ready to sing his praises.

2) **2 Cor. 1:18-22.** God doesn't "sit on the fence" wondering whether or not to save men. As Paul affirms, he has said "Yes" to man and his world through Christ Jesus.

3) **Mk. 2:1-12.** In the Gospels of the past several Sundays, we have heard of Jesus' power over pain, sickness, and evil. Today Mark shows us that Jesus as Messiah can also forgive sin.

HOMILY NOTES:

● The Kingdom that Christ preached is essentially a freeing of man from sin and its consequences, sickness and death. Isaiah foretold that the coming of the Messiah would mean just that. Jesus' progress through Galilee demonstrated it.

● His miracles are signs of the presence of God among us, not simply acts of compassion or wonder-working. The paralytic man suffered from spiritual paralysis as well as bodily sickness, but Christ freed him from both. Now life can begin again for him.

● We do not yet see the world free from sickness and death; the Kingdom, though begun, is not achieved. It will be achieved when Christ's love is shown by all his followers and creation is gathered together under Christ as head.

GENERAL INTERCESSIONS:

Invitation: Through Baptism we have been anointed with the same Spirit which anointed Jesus for his work as Messiah. Our lives have, therefore, the same purpose as Christ's had: to bring wholeness to men torn apart by illness and sin. Let us pray for the strength to carry out this purpose, as we respond: **LORD, FILL US WITH YOUR SPIRIT.**

1. That the Spirit may guide the Church in its mission to preach the forgiveness of sins to all who seek God's mercy, we pray to the Lord.

2. That we may foster peace in the hearts of men by our readiness to forget and forgive past offenses, we . . .

3. That our presence at this Eucharist may be a sign of our dedication to carry on Christ's work even in routine, daily tasks, we . . .

4. For those who seek to mend the shattered lives of human beings through research in medicine and psychiatry, we . . .

5. For the retarded, and for those who provide physical and educational therapy for them, we . . .

*(Additional invocations)*_____

Conclusion: Pour forth your healing Spirit, Father, on the wounds and divisions of our world. Enlighten our eyes and our hearts: do not let us close them to men who need a word of hope and encouragement. For, in this as in all things, we long to be the instruments of your merciful love, through Christ our Lord.

ADDITIONAL INVITATION TO COMMUNION:

Behold the Son of Man who forgives our sins!

PRAYER AFTER COMMUNION:

"God has anointed us, marking us with his seal and giving us the pledge, the Spirit, that we carry in our hearts." Anointed by the one Spirit and united by sharing one bread, let us pray for the unity of all mankind in the peace of Christ.

Eighth Sunday of the Year

THEME: STARTING A NEW LIFE

INTRODUCTION:

Sometimes intense personal grief becomes the occasion for an insight into God's mercy. Such was the case of the prophet Hosea, whose love for an unfaithful wife revealed something of God's steadfast love for his people. The Lord doesn't hold grudges; he is always ready to give men a fresh start on a new life. The first Christians called this process of starting a new life with God "conversion." Conversion means a revolutionary change of heart and mind; it means also that we have to give others the chance to start believing and loving again.

INVITATION TO PENITENTIAL RITE:

My friends, God is not a cosmic computer who keeps strict tabs on our every misdemeanor; he is a Father more interested in showing compassion than in nagging us for our faults. Let us ask ourselves if we have not, now and then, been too willing to condemn and too stingy in forgiving the faults of others.

FORM C: *(Optional invocations)*

From moment to moment you crown our lives with love and compassion: Lord, have mercy.

From day to day give us the chance to start a new life: Christ . . .

From age to age you speak to the hearts of men: Lord . . .

OPENING PRAYER:

Let us pray, pledging ourselves to hear God's Word according to the Spirit which brings life.

READINGS:

1) **Hos. 2:16-17, 21-22.** Hosea did not abandon his wife even when she proved faithless. And God reacts to his people in similar fashion: he will continue to keep his covenant with them in tenderness and love.

2) **2 Cor. 3:1-6.** For Paul the real proof of his ministry for Christ lay not in written letters, but in the hearts of the people he served.

3) **Mk. 2:18-22.** The Christian Gospel is always new — new wine for new wineskins. This gives us confidence that, no matter what our past lives have been like, we can always start fresh again with Christ.

HOMILY NOTES:

● The prophet Hosea had an unfaithful wife, but instead of divorcing her, he pursued her and won her back to his love. Hosea's wife stands for unfaithful Israel whom God lured back, and also for us.

● As we return to God, we experience anew the tenderness of his constant love; we start life anew. This new life must not be a patched-up affair; we must put on a garment made of whole new cloth.

● No one puts new wine into old wineskins — the fermentation would burst the skins. Our new way of life cannot be fitted into the old pattern of things; we must make a radical change, and start afresh.

GENERAL INTERCESSIONS:

Invitation: In the book of Revelation, St. John hears Christ saying "Behold, I make all things new." Such is the power of the risen Lord in our midst: he can pick up the pieces of our shattered lives and help us start living again. Let us pray that we may be open to the Lord's new work in us, as we respond: **GRANT US NEW LIFE.**

1. That the Church may always be refreshed and renewed by the new wine of the Gospel, we pray to the Lord.

2. That we may contribute actively to changes in the Church's life and worship which are necessary if our world is to hear the message of Christ's Gospel, we . . .

3. That Christians may affirm the holiness of work by seeking just wages and better working conditions for all who labor, we . . .

4. That God may bless Christian marriages with happiness and fidelity, we . . .

5. For people who are trying to get a new start in life, especially the newly married, those just graduated from high school and college, those newly released from hospitals and prisons, we . . .

*(Additional invocations)*_____

Conclusion: Father, with each new day you give us the chance to start living for you again. Guide us by your Spirit as we go forward to bring men the message of a Gospel that always remains fresh and new. We make our prayer through Christ our Lord.

ADDITIONAL INVITATION TO COMMUNION:

Behold the Lord who crowns our lives with compassion and love!

PRAYER AFTER COMMUNION:

Paul wrote to the Corinthians: "Ours is not a covenant of written letters but of the Spirit: the written letters bring death, but the Spirit gives life." Let us pray for a faith that is not based on laws and prescriptions, but on the Spirit who offers us new life each day.

Ninth Sunday of the Year

THEME: SUNDAY WORSHIP

INTRODUCTION:

The Gospel for this Sunday's Mass urges us to examine our real motives for worshipping. When Jesus challenged the duplicity of the Scribes and Pharisees, he did not accuse them of failure to worship — this they did *religiously* — but he charged them with having their priorities all wrong. Worship makes sense, Jesus asserted, only if it is the product of a life spent in service. Otherwise worship is a formality, a cheap attempt to salve one's conscience for the glaring failure of our relations with other people. The old rabbinic saying which Jesus quotes still hits home: "The sabbath was made for man, not man for the sabbath."

INVITATION TO PENITENTIAL RITE:

Nothing wrecks prayer and worship more totally than an attitude of smugness and self-justification. In simple honesty let us open our hearts to God and confess those times we have been all too ready to cast stones and hurl condemnations at people whose actions we don't understand.

FORM C: *(Optional invocations)*

You came, a light shining in our darkness: Lord, have mercy.

You taught that respect for life is more important than fulfilling laws: Christ . . .

You died so that your life could be manifest in our mortal flesh: Lord . . .

OPENING PRAYER:

Let us pray that our worship here today may be the sign of lives devoted to the salvation of others.

READINGS:

1) **Dt. 5:12-15.** It is important to notice, in our reading from Deuteronomy, that the sabbath rest was given for the good of *all* creatures — even the ox and the donkey! For us life means more than work; it also means thanksgiving and simple joy in the good things of earth.

2) **2 Cor. 4:6-11.** Paul writes that we can never despair if we remember that the life of Jesus shines in us even when we feel "down and out."

3) **Mk. 2:23—3:6.** Today's reading from Mark reports the last of a series of controversies between Jesus and his opponents. In this selection Jesus maintains the principle that religious laws should serve human needs — not vice versa.

HOMILY NOTES:

● "The sabbath was made for man," something given to man for his good. By whom? By God. "Observe the sabbath day, keep it holy, as the Lord God commanded." What is the sabbath? A set of rules? Christ seems to have swept these aside.

● Is the sabbath a hang-over from the Old Law which Christ abolished we re-introduced? Christ perfected it for us. "We hold our treasure in earthen vessels: the need to recollect and to return to the sources of our Christian vocation is always there. The busier we are, the greater the need to pause and take stock. Particularly is this true of those engaged in the direct apostolate, whether priests, teachers, religious, missionaries or lay people.

● "For while we live we are always being given up to death for Jesus' sake, so that the life of Jesus may be made manifest in our mortal flesh." Now we see what the Christian sabbath is: the death and resurrection of Christ given us by the Father, for the redemption of our mortal lives. We are still commanded to do this "in memory of me."

GENERAL INTERCESSIONS:

Invitation: Throughout his public ministry Jesus consistently fought the idea that persons were mere pawns in a religious chess-game. Let us pray for God's light in recognizing that the good of people should never be sacrificed to a legal system. Our response is:

LORD, SHINE IN OUR HEARTS.

1. That our response to the Church's worship may reflect the dignity of mature brothers and sisters in Christ, we pray to the Lord.

2. That in worshipping the God whom we cannot see, we may not forget the needs of the needy brother whom we can see, we . . .

3. That those who work in law and government may consistently place the good of human beings above legalistic concerns, we . . .

4. For all who contribute to our Sunday worship by giving of their time and effort in planning and preparation, we . . .

*(Additional invocations)*_____

Conclusion: Father, you find your delight and glory in men who are fully alive. Help us remember that our love for you is measured by our love for the wretched and afflicted, that you would rather have us save a man's life than ignore or destory it, that you desire mercy and not sacrifice. We make our prayer through Christ our Lord.

ADDITIONAL INVITATION TO COMMUNION:

Behold Jesus, whose life is manifest in our bodies!

PRAYER AFTER COMMUNION:

"Wherever we may be, we carry with us in our body the death of Jesus, so that the life of Jesus, too, may always be seen in our body." Conscious that we carry within our hearts the hope of the world, let us pray for strength to communicate Christ's presence to every living person.

Tenth Sunday of the Year

THEME: THE DARK FORCE OF EVIL

INTRODUCTION:

In recent years our literature and films reflect a renewed interest in the occult, the demonic, the forces of savage evil. Some of this interest has, of course, been superstitious; yet some of it deserves to be taken seriously by Christians. The experience of systematic human slaughter in wars, as well as senseless acts of violence in our own country, should make us reflect deeply on the way evil makes its presence felt in contemporary society. In Mark's Gospel particularly, Jesus is often portrayed as an "exorcist," one who drives out the power of evil by his life, death, and resurrection. We are called to cooperate with Christ in the work of eliminating cruelty and evil in our own lives and in those of our brothers.

INVITATION TO PENITENTIAL RITE:

As brothers and sisters of Jesus we have the task of opposing whatever stands in the way of God's Kingdom of justice and peace. Before we eat of Christ's Supper, let us recall the ways we have cooperated with the powers of evil by our cowardice in failing to speak out against violence and cruelty.

FORM C: *(Optional invocations)*

Your life was a battle against those forces which enslave men: Lord, have mercy.

Your cross broke the power of evil and destroyed death: Christ . . .

Your resurrection gives us hope that evil will be conquered in us as well: Lord . . .

OPENING PRAYER:

Ours is an age when so many forces compete for our allegiance that it is often difficult to know exactly what God expects of us. Let us pray for the wisdom to discover and follow God's will.

READINGS:

1) **Gn. 3:9-15.** The third chapter of Genesis provides a striking account of the way sin corrodes the relationships between God and man, and among men themselves. But we are also given a hint of God's promise of future redemption.

2) **2 Cor. 4:13—5:1.** The hardships Paul endured in his apostleship were tolerable because of his belief that God will raise us up to life with Christ. Paul's faith is also our own.

3) **Mk. 3:20-35.** Jesus was misunderstood and opposed by the very persons one might have thought would accept him — his own relatives and the religious leaders of his people. His real brothers and sisters, Jesus asserts, are those who do the Father's will.

HOMILY NOTES:

● Who can claim to be brothers and sisters of Jesus Christ? Those, he says, who try to do the will of his Father. But there are powers at large in the world, as well as within us, working to prevail on us to break or reject this relationship with Jesus.

● The "serpent, the beast accursed beyond all wild beasts" of the first reading stands for those satanic powers. So does "Beelzebub" of the Gospel reading. These forces are called elsewhere in Scripture the "spirits of wickedness in high places," "the devil," the "roaring lion seeking out its prey," the "powers of darkness."

● The preposterous image of a tailed devil brandishing a pitchfork has helped to make many people believe that the words "devil," "demon," or "satanism" have little or no content. Jesus certainly thought of them as implacable, dynamic enemies and had to experience the accusation that he was motivated by the very evil he fought against.

● The Gospel shows that he overcame these enemies. He offers us also the means of resistance. It is the one he used — obedience to the will of his Father.

GENERAL INTERCESSIONS:

Invitation: Our struggle against the forces of evil will be successful to the degree we unite ourselves in prayer, work, and worship with Christ. Knowing this, let us offer our petitions to the Father, as we respond: **LORD, YOUR WILL BE DONE.**

1. That we may give wholehearted support to the Church's struggle against those dark forces that enslave men to violence and crime, we pray to the Lord.

2. That as Christians we may be vocal in our criticism of those who exploit men through political pressure and corrupt business practices, we . . .

3. That we may discover God's will for us and have the courage to follow it, we . . .

4. For persons who suffer misunderstanding and rejection by those they love most deeply, we . . .

*(Additional invocations)*_____

Conclusion: Father, we pray that you will deliver us from the power of evil, especially the evil we are too blind or too cowardly to recognize. Complete in us your Son's work of healing and deliverance, and make us true brothers and sisters of him whom you raised from death. We make our prayer through the same Christ our Lord.

ADDITIONAL INVITATION TO COMMUNION:

Behold Jesus our brother, who came to do the Father's will!

PRAYER AFTER COMMUNION:

The Lord said in his Gospel: "Anyone who does the will of God, that person is my brother and sister and mother." Let us pray for strength to resist those forces which prevent us from seeking and doing God's will for our salvation.

Eleventh Sunday of the Year

THEME: GROWTH

INTRODUCTION:

One of the major themes of the Bible concerns the way God brings fruitfulness and growth out of what appears to be sterile and insignificant. Examples of this theme abound: Abraham and Sarah are given a child in their old age; a miserable group of slaves in Egypt are chosen as God's people Israel; Jesus, the carpenter's son from Nazareth, is revealed as Messiah and Lord. But the *growth* God gives is not divine magic; it always requires the responsible cooperation of human beings. Today's Gospel parable about the mustard seed gives us the chance to reflect on the growth God gives and the part we play in it.

INVITATION TO PENITENTIAL RITE:

Growth is such a natural, normal phenomenon that we often don't notice it — until it stops. The same thing can happen in a life of faith: we can gradually become estranged from God almost without noticing it. Let us examine our hearts to see if this is happening to us.

FORM C: *(Optional invocations)*

We confess our failings, confident of your steadfast love: Lord, have
    mercy.

We thirst for you, the fountain of living water: Christ . . .

We long for the full revelation of your kingdom in us: Lord . . .

OPENING PRAYER:

Let us pray that we may become mature Christians through our cooperation with the growth of God's life in us.

READINGS:

1) **Ez. 17:22-24.** Our selection from the prophet Ezekiel was chosen because it describes the spread of God's Kingdom as the growth of a tree that provides shade for all creatures — a theme found also in today's Gospel.

2) **2 Cor. 5:6-10.** Whatever our circumstances in life, Paul remarks, we should be intent upon one thing only: pleasing the Lord.

3) **Mk. 4:26-34.** The chief point about Jesus' parables concerning the growth of the Kingdom seems to be the spectacular contrast between small beginnings and great results. The Kingdom is sown in human hearts as a tiny seed, but grows into a transforming tree of life.

HOMILY NOTES:

● There are two fascinating things about growth. One is the potential in something as insignificant as a seed or a cutting. The other is the mysterious process of growth itself.

● The people who heard Christ tell the parable of the mustard seed could see little evidence of anything significant being achieved by a small group of obscure men who, starting with their leader, nearly all came to a bad end. It is the twentieth-century Christian who is aware of the truth of his words.

● What is hard to realize is that the growth is still going on and we are involved. Each of us is like a plant in process of becoming the individual God wants us to be. Each of us is also like a farmer contributing to the harvest of what God wants the world to be.

● On both levels, because of our unique place in the hierarchy of nature, we are obliged to make decisions about how much we will co-operate with God.

GENERAL INTERCESSIONS:

Invitation: Man is unique because he can grow on so many different levels at once — physical, emotional, spiritual. Let us pray that Christ will guide us as we grow into mature citizens of his Kingdom. Our response is: **YOUR KINGDOM COME.**

1. That the Church may continue to grow in holiness through prayer and active charity, we pray to the Lord.

2. That our contact with God's living Word in worship may open our eyes to the growing presence of his Kingdom in the world, we ...

3. That we may receive from this Eucharist the nourishment we need to mature in faith, in hope and in love, we ...

4. That parents may help their children grow in that human freedom which fosters the life of the Spirit, we ...

5. For persons whose growth has been stunted by crippling diseases or by emotional disturbances, we ...

*(Additional invocations)*_____

Conclusion: Father, we pray for the coming of your Kingdom on all levels of human existence. May it come as a Kingdom of justice for the oppressed, as a Kingdom of hope for the despairing, as a Kingdom of love for the lonely and unwanted. Above all, may it come as a Kingdom of everlasting life for all who trust in you, through Christ our Lord.

ADDITIONAL INVITATION TO COMMUNION:

Behold Christ, in whom the fulness of God's Kingdom dwells!

PRAYER AFTER COMMUNION:

Today we heard Paul saying: "Whether we are living in the body or exiled from it, we are intent on pleasing the Lord." Let us pray that in our busy, active lives we may not neglect their important sources of growth — prayer and service to one another.

Twelfth Sunday of the Year

THEME: FAITH IN TIME OF TROUBLE

INTRODUCTION:

The problem of human suffering is as old as man himself. Wise men of all ages have sought solutions; but none of them prove wholly satisfactory — nor do they alleviate the suffering itself, as the Old Testament figure Job discovered. Christianity does not claim a neat answer to the question of pain, but it does bring new meaning to human suffering by viewing it in relation to Jesus' own dying and rising. The trials and troubles of a Christian — like those of Jesus — are the birth pangs of a powerful new life, which will one day transform the world into a new creation.

INVITATION TO PENITENTIAL RITE:

Although pain is inevitable in human life, it does not have to be totally absurd and meaningless. In fact, our own difficulties can inspire us to provide comfort and assistance to others in pain and sorrow. Let us ask ourselves if we have been so concerned about our own trials that we have ignored the suffering of others.

FORM C: *(Optional invocations)*

Sharing our weakness and suffering, you taught us compassion: Lord, have mercy.
Accepting the pain of the Cross, you led us to a new life: Christ . . .
Rising in glory, you sent the Spirit to console us in time of trouble: Lord . . .

OPENING PRAYER:

Let us pray that our faith will help us cope with our personal difficulties, and make us more sensitive to the pain of others.

READINGS:

1) **Jb. 38:1, 8-11.** The attitude toward suffering in the Book of Job differs from that expressed by other Old Testament writers. For Job suffering is a mystery which human reasoning cannot grasp. By contrast, other biblical authors felt suffering was the result of sin and rebellion against God.
2) **2 Cor. 5:14-17.** According to Paul, Jesus' suffering, death, and resurrection have made us and our world a new creation. As a result, we live no longer for ourselves, but for Christ and for others.
3) **Mk. 4:35-41.** The purpose of Mark's story about Jesus' calming the storm is to illustrate how the disciples gradually came to understand who Christ was. They discover that he can not only calm storms, but also every human fear.

HOMILY NOTES:

● We frequently have to cope with our own and other people's sufferings. We ask why? Job asks why? The disciples in the boat in the storm ask why? They rush up to Jesus, afraid that unless he wakes up and acts they will be drowned.

● A straight answer to our question is not given us. Job is told that he cannot fathom why God permits suffering. The disciples are told that they cannot drown when Life itself is with them. Christ calls upon us to rely on his power to bring us through any danger, any suffering, any fears, even through death itself, to his Life.

● The experience of suffering may enable us to learn that we cannot hope to live with Christ and participate with him in our Father's transformation of the world, without also suffering and dying with him.

GENERAL INTERCESSIONS:

Invitation: The love of Christ, Paul remarked in our second reading, is so overwhelming that it can transform us into a new creation. Let us pray that this love will give us strength to cope with our own sufferings, and help us assist others who are troubled or in need. Our response is: **LORD, TRANSFORM OUR LIVES.**

1. That those who are embittered by suffering and pain may find a new meaning in life through faith in Christ, we pray to the Lord.

2. That we may always seek reconciliation with our brother before we bring our gifts to the altar, we . . .

3. That Christians may lend support to those international organizations which strive to alleviate human misery through gifts of food and medicine, we . . .

4. That we may show sympathy and understanding to those who are tortured by doubt, we . . .

5. For all who suffer in silence because they are afraid to ask for help, we . . .

*(Additional invocations)*_____

Conclusion: Father, your love revealed in Jesus helps us to live not for ourselves, but for others. Transform our suffering into a source of compassionate sensitivity for those who need our help and support. We make our prayer through Christ our Lord.

ADDITIONAL INVITATION TO COMMUNION:

Behold Christ, who calms every fear!

PRAYER AFTER COMMUNION:

"For anyone who is in Christ, there is a new creation; the old creation is gone, and now the new one is here." Let us pray that our lives of faith and charity may open up new vistas of meaning and value for men who do not yet know the Good News of Christ.

Thirteenth Sunday of the Year

THEME: THE POWER OF LIFE

INTRODUCTION:
We have all read stories of people who survived calamities on land and sea, who went for days without food or water or shelter, until they were finally rescued. Man's will to live is an amazing power; it strongly reflects the power of life in God himself. The author of the Book of Wisdom recognized this when he wrote that God made man imperishable, made him the "image of his own nature." Christ brought a new dimension to life's power by showing that even death has lost its grip on men. For one who believes in Christ, death has been swallowed up by the dynamic power of a risen life.

INVITATION TO PENITENTIAL RITE:
The only thing that can utterly destroy a man is for him to abandon his belief that life has purpose or meaning. Let us seriously ask ourselves if we have destroyed the hope of others by closing our eyes and ears to them when they were struggling to discover some reason for living.

FORM C: *(Optional invocations)*
You created all things good, giving them breath and life: Lord, have mercy.

You re-created us in your image through the waters of Baptism: Christ . . .

You restored life to the dead by the power of your resurrection: Lord . . .

OPENING PRAYER:
Let us pray, giving thanks that the Father has created and re-created us in Christ Jesus.

READINGS:
1) **Wis. 1:13-15; 2:23-24.** The author of the Book of Wisdom, who wrote only about 50 years before Christ, understood that God wills only one thing for man and for the world: imperishable life.

2) **2 Cor. 8:7, 9, 13-15.** Although Christ was rich, Paul comments, he became poor for our sake. As Christians we are asked to give generously out of our surplus goods to relieve the needy.

3) **Mk. 5:21-43.** The author of our first reading asserted that God takes no pleasure in the death of living things. This point is verified in today's Gospel account which shows Jesus restoring health to a woman with a hemorrhage, and raising a little girl back to life.

HOMILY NOTES:

● The writer of the Book of Wisdom realizes that God wants creation to exist, to live, "to be." God is the dynamic source of life. He created things to live. Creation is essentially good.

● But death is with us every day; we fear the annihilation of it, its finality. But, now that Christ has been through death and been raised, we know that we will be raised, too. He showed he had the power of life, when he raised the little girl, the widow's son, and Lazarus.

● Resurrection with Christ is for those who have died with him. We do not repudiate God's gift of life, but use it to the full, and render to him at death a life of love and service shared with our fellow men.

GENERAL INTERCESSIONS:

Invitation: Since we were created by God to live as fully, happily, and humanly as possible, let us pray for our own needs and those of the entire world. Our response is: **LORD, WE PRAISE YOUR GOODNESS.**

1. That we may spend this Lord's Day in thankful gratitude for the beauty and goodness of created things, we pray to the Lord.

2. That we may follow Paul's advice in sharing our surplus goods with others who have need of them, we . . .

3. That we may cooperate with those who labor to provide clean air and water, so that our communities will be healthier places to live, we . . .

4. That medical science may soon find a cure for those who suffer from rare diseases which prevent them from living full and active lives, we . . .

5. For those in our community who have died recently, that they may enjoy forever the risen life of Jesus, we . . .

*(Additional invocations)*_____

Conclusion: Father, we thank you for changing our mourning into dancing, our tears into joy. As images of your goodness, we praise your loving care of the world, and we ask that you grant all men lives that are as happy and fully human as possible, through Christ our Lord.

ADDITIONAL INVITATION TO COMMUNION:

Behold the Lord Jesus who, though rich, became poor for our sake!

PRAYER AFTER COMMUNION:

Jesus said to the woman of today's Gospel: "My daughter, your faith has restored you to health; go in peace." As we have been touched by Jesus' healing power in this Eucharist, let us pray that all men may become fully alive to God's loving care for them.

Fourteenth Sunday of the Year

THEME: PROPHETS

INTRODUCTION:

Just who are prophets and what do they do? That is a question posed by today's liturgy. First, perhaps, we need to get rid of some stereotyped images: not all prophets wear animal skins and live in caves; nor are all of them abnormal; nor do all of them predict the future. In fact, the main function of the prophet is to reveal to his contemporaries what God is doing in their midst *at this present moment.* In this sense, Ezekiel, Paul, and Jesus were all prophets: they pointed to God's action here and now — even when many people preferred to ignore it. We might well ask ourselves who the prophets of today are.

INVITATION TO PENITENTIAL RITE:

My brothers and sisters, one of the most painful tasks in life is to have to tell someone things you know he doesn't want to hear. Yet that is often the duty of a prophet — a duty that Christians, as a prophetic people, also have. How often have we neglected to speak the truth of Christ because of laziness or fear?

FORM C: *(Optional invocations)*

Though you give us the message of truth, we often stop our ears:
   Lord, have mercy.

Though you reveal the Father's will, we often shut our eyes:
   Christ . . .

Though you call us to repentance, we often close our hearts:
   Lord . . .

OPENING PRAYER:

Let us pray that our hearts may be open to those who are prophets of God's action among us today.

READINGS:

1) **Ez. 2:2-5.** This passage from Ezekiel was selected because of its relation to today's Gospel. Even though men are defiant and rebellious, God keeps sending his prophets to preach faith and repentance.

2) **2 Cor. 12:7-10.** Paul's life was a perfect example of what it means to be a prophet: human weakness becomes evidence of Christ's power to save.

3) **Mk. 6:1-6.** Like the Old Testament prophets before him, Jesus experiences the bitter fact of rejection and misunderstanding. As Paul once said, Jesus' prophetic life and crucifixion will always be a scandal for those who refuse to believe.

HOMILY NOTES:

● Throughout Jewish history the theme of rejection is continually found. God sent his prophets to instruct the people and each in turn was rejected, many of them being ill-treated, even killed.

● When Christ came journeying through Judea and Galilee, he was acclaimed with enthusiasm by all until he came to his native Nazareth, where he was regarded as a presumptuous upstart by his fellow citizens. Where did this man get all this? What is this wisdom that has been granted him? We know all his relations, what can we learn from him? Because of their closed minds, Christ could make no impression on them.

● The prophets God has chosen have always been unlikely people from a human standpoint. We must be open and receptive to the truth from whatever source it may come.

GENERAL INTERCESSIONS:

Invitation: Psalm 95 (94) contains a phrase we all need to take seriously: "Today, if you hear his voice, do not harden your hearts." Let us pray especially for openness to God's truth wherever and however it may be revealed to us. Our response is: **LORD, OPEN OUR HEARTS.**

1. That, guided by the Holy Spirit, the Church may remain true to its prophetic mission of interpreting God's truth and action in the world, we pray to the Lord.

2. That we may watch attentively for God revealing himself in our ordinary work and our personal relationships, we . . .

3. That we may learn to listen as closely to God's Word in creation and Scripture as we listen to human words on radio and television, we . . .

4. That we may never despise the poor and the weak, since in them Christ often reveals his life and salvation, we . . .

5. For persons who are bitter and disillusioned because they feel no one understands them, we . . .

(Additional invocations)_____

Conclusion: Open our hearts, Father, to your life-giving Word. Forgive us the times we have refused to listen to your truth, and grant us that kind of humble weakness that permits the power of Jesus to govern our lives. We make our prayer through the same Christ our Lord.

ADDITIONAL INVITATION TO COMMUNION:

Behold Christ, the prophet who speaks only the truth of God!

PRAYER AFTER COMMUNION:

Paul wrote: "I shall be very happy to make my weaknesses my special boast, so that the power of Christ may stay over me." Let us pray, opening our hearts to the strength Christ gives, even when we feel weak, contemptible, and depressed.

Fifteenth Sunday of the Year

THEME: MISSION

INTRODUCTION:

Becoming a servant of God and of men is decidedly not like winning a popularity contest. The prophet Amos knew that; so did Paul, and so did Jesus and the apostles. We can cooperate in the mission of bringing all creation to the truth and freedom of God's plan only because we were first chosen in Christ, chosen, as Paul tells us today, "before the world began . . . to be holy and spotless, and to live through love in his presence."

INVITATION TO PENITENTIAL RITE:

Our mission as Christians is to free men to the highest possible degree for a constructive life of service. As we begin our Eucharist, let us ask ourselves this question: Do we really allow God's plan to take hold of our lives, or do we confine our Christianity to a few bored moments at Sunday liturgy?

FORM C: *(Optional invocations)*

Your blood gains us freedom and forgiveness: Lord, have mercy.
Your resurrection brings everything in heaven and on earth to-
gether: Christ . . .
Your Spirit seals us in truth and love: Lord . . .

OPENING PRAYER:

Let us pray that the mystery of God's love revealed in Christ may become the deepest meaning of our personal lives, and the source of our mission in the world.

READINGS:

1) **Am. 7:12-15.** Amos lived as a shepherd in the eighth century before Christ. His mission illustrates the common biblical notion that a man's call to prophesy is not based on personal whim but on God's initiative.

2) **Eph. 1:3-14.** Paul sings of the mystery of God's purpose for our salvation: before the world was made we were chosen to live through love in his presence.

3) **Mk. 6:7-13.** After spending time with Jesus, hearing his wisdom and witnessing his mighty work, the Twelve are sent out to assume their share in the ministry of healing and preaching repentance.

HOMILY NOTES:

• In the Old Testament the prophets denounced the false and callous shepherds, who failed in their task of leading the people. God, they were convinced, would intervene one day. "I will set shepherds over them, who will care for them," said Jeremiah, speaking for God.

● The time came when God sent a shepherd who did truly care for the people, his son Jesus. He had compassion on the people because they were like sheep without a shepherd. And his care was not only for Israel; it extended to the whole of mankind.

● Today we have the task of continuing Christ's work, of bringing his care and compassion to others. This is a time of unprecedented joint responsibility in the Church, and we share with our bishops the pastoral responsibility of revealing Christ to all men "near and far off."

GENERAL INTERCESSIONS:

Invitation: We were claimed in Christ as God's very own sons and daughters, and we are challenged to match that claim by a personal decision to serve. Let us rededicate ourselves in prayer to continue Christ's mission in the world, as we respond: **LORD, ALL GLORY BE YOURS.**

1. That pastors and people may be open to one another's insights as they work together to carry on Christ's work of serving human needs, we pray to the Lord.

2. That Christian families may drink in the wisdom of God's plan for salvation through their prayer, worship, and work together, we . . .

3. That we may work to build up Christ's Kingdom by seeking improvements in the conditions under which men of our day must live and work, we . . .

4. That our commitment to activity for the Church may not dull our hearts to the need for periods of silence, prayer, and reflection, we . . .

5. For young people who are searching for ways to combine their desire for freedom with a mature sense of responsibility, we . . .

*(Additional invocations)*_____

Conclusion: Blessed are you, Father, for you chose us in Christ to be your very own people. Fill us, we pray, with the wisdom and insight that will lead to holiness and everlasting life in your presence, so that all creation may one day sing a hymn to your glory, through Christ our Lord.

ADDITIONAL INVITATION TO COMMUNION:

Behold Christ, the head of all things in heaven and on earth!

PRAYER AFTER COMMUNION:

"Now you, too, in Christ, have heard the message of the truth and the good news of your salvation." Let us pray that, as the apostles were sent forth to continue Christ's work, we may fulfill that same mission among people of our own time and place.

Sixteenth Sunday of the Year

THEME: CHRIST'S PASTORAL WORK

INTRODUCTION:

In regard to the pastoral ministry of priests, Vatican II stated: "They gather God's family together as a brotherhood of living unity, and lead it through Christ and in the Spirit to God the Father" *(Decree on Ministry and Life of Priests, #6)*. It is significant that similar language was used in commenting on the vocation of married couples: they become "witnesses of the mystery of that love which the Lord revealed to the world by his dying and his rising to life again" *(Church in the Modern World, #52)*. These words invite us all to reflect on our common responsibility to unite men in loving faith by continuing the pastoral activity of Jesus.

INVITATION TO PENITENTIAL RITE:

In today's second reading, we will hear Paul telling us that Christ has broken down all the barriers that separate men from God and from one another. Let us reflect on the ways we have damaged the unity of Christ's body by building up barriers of misunderstanding and resentment.

FORM C: *(Optional invocations)*

We have been brought close to the Father through your blood: Lord, have mercy.

We are at peace with one another through your sacrifice: Christ . . .

We have access to the Father in the one Spirit: Lord . . .

OPENING PRAYER:

Let us pray that we may work together peacefully in the pastoral mission of building up the Body of Christ.

READINGS:

1) **Jer. 23:1-6.** Once again the Old Testament reading serves as prelude and commentary for the Gospel. Jeremiah looks forward to a time when the remnant of God's People will be cared for by shepherds who seek truth and justice more than personal gain. The shepherd theme in the Gospel will illustrate how Christ fulfills this prophecy.

2) **Eph. 2:13-18.** Christ brought the Good News of peace and re-conciliation to all men. For this reason, Paul reflects, Christ is the New Man who restores the unity lost by sin and death.

3) **Mk. 6:30-34.** Jesus' love and attention to ordinary people is beautifully depicted in our passage from Mark's Gospel. We can see in Christ the fulfillment of Jeremiah's vision of a shepherd full of wisdom, honesty, and integrity.

HOMILY NOTES:

● Our instinct on hearing a piece of good news is to share it with everyone: no one keeps it to himself. Our Christian faith is good news too, more vital than any other, but we often behave as if only professional missionaries were to hand it on.

● For many people their mission is to their immediate neighbors and workmates. Others God requires to uproot themselves, like Amos, or like the apostles sent out to preach. God's plan is to bring all creation under the rule of Christ.

● The Christian's mission is to use his technology and labor to improve the lot of man on earth, to raise men's living standards to those fit for brothers of Christ. Men freed from the crushing burden of hunger and disease and death can more readily find faith in a loving Savior.

GENERAL INTERCESSIONS:

Invitation: The ministry of Jesus was marked by concern for basic human needs; he never tried to escape the ordinary cares of people, but instead he worked as they did, sharing their thoughts, their way of living, their joys and sadness. Let us commit ourselves to a similar style of ministry, as we pray: **LORD, GRANT US YOUR PEACE.**

1. That pastors in the Church may live in such a way as to manifest their concern for the ordinary needs and goals of their people, we pray to the Lord.

2. That, as Church, we may be guided by the Spirit in our ministry of preaching the truth that can make men free, we . . .

3. That nations may seek a solution for their conflicts through peaceful dialogue rather than through the mutual slaughter of war, we . . .

4. That we may take steps to help those who lack the basic human needs of food, clothing, and shelter, we . . .

5. That sinners may find in the sacrament of Penance a source of peace, of reconciliation with God and their neighbors, we . . .

*(Additional invocations)*_____

Conclusion: Father, help us become effective witnesses to your truth and your love which have saved the world. Fill us with peace, with the Spirit of reconciliation, and with the courage to make whatever sacrifices are necessary to care for the needs of those your Son redeemed by his blood. We make our prayer though the same Chist our Lord.

ADDITIONAL INVITATION TO COMMUNION:

Behold Christ who restored peace through his blood on the cross!

PRAYER AFTER COMMUNION:

Speaking of Christ, Paul wrote: "He is the peace between us." United in peace by sharing in Christ's table, let us pray that all men may enjoy the unity of the Spirit which leads to the Father.

Seventeenth Sunday of the Year

THEME: GOD'S POWER AND OUR FAITH

INTRODUCTION:
Of all creatures man alone is capable of making free decisions which affect the direction and development of his life and his world. Without this ability to make free choices, man's faith would be meaningless. Our faith works in cooperation with God's power to save and provide for critical human needs. God is powerful not because he works miracles "at the drop of a hat," but because he calls forth in us the sturdy faith we need to choose those values and actions which will contribute to the world's betterment.

INVITATION TO PENITENTIAL RITE:
Although it is true that God's power sustains human life, it is equally true that we must use our ingenuity in caring for others. Let us ask ourselves if at times we have appealed to God's creative power as an excuse for avoiding the difficult work of caring for persons in need.

FORM C: *(Optional invocations)*
You are close to all who call on you from their hearts: Lord, have
  mercy.
You make us a people through one faith and one Baptism: Christ . . .
You feed and nourish us by your Word and your Body: Lord . . .

OPENING PRAYER:
Let us pray for a faith humble enough to trust God's providence and courageous enough to move mountains.

READINGS:
1) **2 Kgs. 4:42-44.** God's concern for man is not limited to spiritual values and accomplishments. Our reading from the Second Book of Kings shows that God cares intensely for the physical well-being of persons, too.
2) **Eph. 4:1-6.** Since we Christians share one faith and one Baptism, Paul encourages us to "preserve the unity of the Spirit," through the peace that binds us all together.
3) **Jn. 6:1-15.** Today and for the next four Sundays we hear Jesus' discourse on the Bread of Life from John's Gospel. The bread Christ gives is not only the Eucharist, but also the bread of his teaching and his concern for ordinary human needs.

HOMILY NOTES:
● A simple people like the Israelites saw the direct hand of God in anything out of the way or extraordinary, whereas we are very eager not to credit God with intervening, for fear of appearing ignorant or superstitious.

- The Jewish crowd made the mistake of regarding the miracle in today's Gospel as only a miraculous provision for their material needs. We make the opposite mistake by seeing it only as a sign of the Eucharist, and so we miss the point of Jesus' real compassion for the hunger of the crowd.
- If we understand the Eucharist, we must understand its consequences, that Christ's love has to be put into practice in our ordinary lives. We must care deeply that the people are in need, hungry. The sheer size of social problems demands a faith capable of mountain-moving.
- We should not be afraid to ask for a miracle if we are doing the utmost our human power can manage.

GENERAL INTERCESSIONS:

Invitation: Christians of the rich nations could, if they cared deeply enough and worked together, bring about the end of hunger in the world. Let us ask God to bring to us the responsibility which is ours because we share in the Eucharist. Our response is: **LORD, INCREASE OUR FAITH.**

1. That as Christians we may be filled with the same concern Jesus had for the tired, the hungry, the sick, and the overworked, we pray to the Lord.

2. That in a world which often depends on violence to achieve its goals we may witness to the values of patience, gentleness, and selfless love, we . . .

3. That God's powerful grace may put an end to the scandal of divisions among those who believe in Christ, we . . .

4. That orphans and widows may discover in us a revelation of God's tender love for them, we . . .

5. For good crops and bountiful harvests, especially in those regions of the world that suffer severe shortages of food, we . . .

*(Additional invocations)*_____

Conclusion: Father, your Son was concerned not only for our life in the Spirit, but also for our ordinary human needs of hunger and thirst. Instead of offering the poor only words and noble sentiments, help us to offer them the food and drink they need to lead decent lives, through Christ our Lord.

ADDITIONAL INVITATION TO COMMUNION:

Behold the Lord who feeds the world by his goodness!

PRAYER AFTER COMMUNION:

Let us listen again to Paul's advice: "Bear with one another charitably, in complete selflessness, gentleness, and patience." Let us pray, promising the Father that we will do everything in our power this week to preserve the unity of the Spirit in the bond of peace.

Eighteenth Sunday of the Year

THEME: THE BREAD WE SHARE

INTRODUCTION:

Every expectant mother knows that when she eats food, she does so not only to preserve her own life, but to help give life to the child she carries. It is much the same with our sharing in the Eucharistic bread. We eat the food that nourishes Christ's life in us so that we can communicate that same life to the world in which we work and live.

INVITATION TO PENITENTIAL RITE:

As we prepare to celebrate this covenant meal, let us recall that our faith in Christ's Eucharistic presence will not mean much if we refuse to see him also in the persons of our brothers and sisters.

FORM C: *(Optional invocations)*

Bread of God that comes down from heaven: Lord, have mercy.
Bread of truth that renews us in goodness and holiness: Christ...
Bread of life that feeds our hunger and satisfies our thirst: Lord...

OPENING PRAYER:

Let us pray that Christ's word and bread will not only give us life, but strengthen us to give others a richer life.

READINGS:

1) **Ex. 16:2-4, 12-15.** The bread God provided for Israel in the wilderness was understood by the early Christians as a foreshadowing of that Bread of Life which Christ would give.

2) **Eph. 4:17, 20-24.** Everything about Christian life, Paul suggests, is radically new. Christians have been caught up in a "spiritual revolution" that causes them to assume a personality, a "new self" modeled on the truth of Jesus.

3) **Jn. 6:24-35.** Jesus fulfills the promises of the Old Testament. As Son of Man he gives a living bread which can satisfy our human longing for intimacy and truth.

HOMILY NOTES:

● We need food to live. If we don't eat, we die. In this Eucharistic celebration we will be thanking God together for "this bread, the fruit of the earth and the work of men's hands which will become for us the Bread of Life."

● "This is not the bread of our natural life (which is also the gift of God). This is the Living Bread, Christ himself, which feeds our life in him. In the desert, manna saved the Israelites from death, but that gift of God foreshadowed his greater gift of the Eucharist.

● In the Eucharist we eat this bread from heaven and so share Christ's own life. So our life must therefore be a life like his, one of loving and giving. If Christ feeds us, we must feed him, the Christ who lives in our hungry fellowmen.

● How can a Christian share in the Eucharist and be unconcerned about hunger? The concern we should have should be expressed in our individual giving, and in working to build a body of public opinion that will not allow waste of resources, unjust terms of trade between rich and poor nations, and "aid" which helps the donor at the expense of the receiver.

● This concern must begin now, here, as we go away from the table where Christ feeds us. He must not be able to say to us, "I was hungry and you gave me nothing to eat."

GENERAL INTERCESSIONS:

Invitation: Every day we ask "Give us this day our daily bread." God put the distribution of the world's bread into the hands of men. Let us ask him that, each time we receive the bread from heaven, he reminds us of our responsibility in seeing that the hungry are fed. Our response is: **LORD, GIVE US THE BREAD WE NEED.**

1. That, as a pilgrim Church, we may seek nourishment for our journey to the Father in the bread of Christ's word and the bread of his body, we pray to the Lord.

2. That, as we recognize the Lord in the breaking of bread, we may also see his presence in the hungry poor, the homeless, and the stranger, we . . .

3. That we may give of our time, concern, and material resources to those in real need, without expecting anything in return, we . . .

4. That the Eucharist, as a bond of unity, may strengthen families to overcome their tensions and disagreements, we . . .

5. That our share in the Bread of Life may transform us into new persons who seek, above all, the goodness and holiness of truth, we . . .

*(Additional invocations)*_____

Conclusion: Father, you have taught us that living faith consists in coming to the aid and comfort of those in need. May the bread we share at this table be a sign of our love for you and for all who hunger and thirst after a better life. We make our prayer through Christ our Lord.

ADDITIONAL INVITATION TO COMMUNION:

Behold the Living Bread, given for the life of the world!

PRAYER AFTER COMMUNION:

"I am the bread of life: he who comes to me will never be thirsty; he who believes in me will never thirst." As we have sought and found the living Christ at this table, let us pray that we may also find him among those persons and places where his presence is not so obvious.

Nineteenth Sunday of the Year

THEME: FOOD FOR THE JOURNEY

INTRODUCTION:

The word "companion" literally means "one with whom we share bread." As Christians we are truly companions, because we share a comomn table and a common journey. Just as the bread given the prophet Elijah strengthened him for the journey to God's mountain, so our bread — the flesh of Christ given for the life of the world — strengthens us on our pilgrimage to the Father.

INVITATION TO PENITENTIAL RITE:

One of the finest summaries of Christian life is to be found in Paul's words to the Ephesians: "Be friends with one another, and kind, forgiving each other as readily as God forgave you in Christ." Does this sound like our normal pattern of living, or are we inclined to hold grudges and harbor anger?

FORM C: *(Optional invocations)*

Friend of sinners, companion of the weak: Lord, have mercy.
Living Bread, life of the world: Christ . . .
Heavenly manna, food for our journey: Lord . . .

OPENING PRAYER:

Let us pray that, as Christ gave his flesh for the life of the world, so we may give our lives to one another by loving as he loved.

READINGS:

1) **1 Kgs. 19:4-8.** The prophet Elijah was half-dead from hunger and exhaustion, but the food God furnished gave him strength to journey forty days and nights. This same theme of a bread which restores life will be heard in today's Gospel.

2) **Eph. 4:30—5:2.** Christian life demands that we forgive one another as freely and as fully as God forgave us in Christ. Failure to do this, Paul remarks, will grieve the Holy Spirit of God.

3) **Jn. 6:41-51.** No one can journey to the Father unless he is strengthened by the living bread of Christ. This bread is our pledge that we shall be raised with Jesus from death to glory.

HOMILY NOTES:

● God provided a meal for Elijah as he was on his journey. He fed the Israelites with manna as they journeyed in the wilderness. He provides us with food on our journey to his Kingdom.

● This food he gives us is more than mere nourishment — it is life itself. The man who eats it will not "die." He feeds us too with his Word. In this celebration of the Eucharist we are twice fed—through his Word in the Scriptures and by his body and blood in Communion.

● As we listen to his Word and eat at his table we pledge ourselves to be more like him, filled by his Spirit, living with his life. "Now I do not live by my own life, but Christ lives in me."

GENERAL INTERCESSIONS:

Invitation: Sometimes our lives get so complicated and confused that we feel the need to sit down and ask ourselves just where we're going and how we're going to get there. Jesus tells us that our real journey is towards the Father; so let us ask for the strength to make it, as we pray: **LORD, BE OUR COMPANION.**

1. That under the guidance of the Holy Spirit the Church may confidently show men the way that leads to the Father through Christ, we pray to the Lord.

2. That the routine cares and burdens of daily life may not blind us to the risen life in Christ, which is the true goal of human existence, we . . .

3. That we may unite ourselves to Christ by loving as totally and as selflessly as he did, we . . .

4. That in moments of anxiety and depression we may find in the Living Bread of Christ the courage to go on, we . . .

5. That our joy at this Eucharistic celebration may also embrace those whose lives are drab, colorless, and friendless, we . . .

*(Additional invocations)*_____

Conclusion: Father, sometimes our progress towards you seems slow and painful, yet we continue to rejoice in hope. Draw us together through bread and through love, so that we may come to you as a people made truly one, through Christ our Lord.

ADDITIONAL INVITATION TO COMMUNION:

Behold Christ, who said: "If anyone eats this bread, he will live forever."

PRAYER AFTER COMMUNION:

"This is the bread that comes down from heaven, so that a man may eat it and not die." Let us pray, giving thanks for the bread that enables us to live as Christ lived, and to love as he loved.

Twentieth Sunday of the Year

THEME: ETERNAL LIFE

INTRODUCTION:

Our culture puts a great premium on the value of being (or appearing to be) young. Modern advertising, in fact, promises eternal youth to anyone who will drink a certain breakfast juice or buy the latest laundry detergent. But, in the long run, everybody knows that youth, as life itself, cannot be purchased. In today's Gospel Jesus does, however, freely offer a bread and a life that will not grow old — a life filled with the Spirit, a life that gives thanks, a life that threatens death itself with destruction. That life is what we celebrate and become in the Eucharist.

INVITATION TO PENITENTIAL RITE:

The basic meaning of "eucharist" is thanksgiving; indeed, in Paul's words, all Christian life means "giving thanks to God who is our Father in the name of our Lord Jesus Christ." Let us recall the times we have adopted a grumbling, pessimistic attitude toward life and worship, an attitude inconsistent with the name of Christian.

FORM C: *(Optional invocations)*

Your flesh is real food, your blood is real drink: Lord, have mercy.
You draw life from the Father and we draw life from you: Christ . . .
Your bread will make us live forever: Lord . . .

OPENING PRAYER:

Let us pray that the Living Bread of the Eucharist will lead us to a new wisdom and a new zest for Christian life.

READINGS:

1) **Prv. 9:1-6.** Our reading from Proverbs personifies Wisdom, who invites us to a festive banquet of meat and wine. As Christians we naturally think of the Eucharistic supper wherein Jesus, the Power and Wisdom of God, gives us life by his own flesh and blood.

2) **Eph. 5:15-20.** Paul counsels us, in this passage from Ephesians, to live as a people filled with the Spirit, filled with thanksgiving.

3) **Jn. 6:51-58.** John shows how Jesus is concerned that his people have not only the bread of daily nourishment and the bread of sound teaching, but also the Living Bread of his body, which gives eternal life to the world.

HOMILY NOTES:

• Sometimes the thought of eternal life is rather depressing, when we think of our kind of humdrum existence as going on forever.

But we can no more understand what life with God is like than a two-year-old can enjoy a game of bridge.

● In the Scriptures, trying to teach a simple people, God described life with him as a marvellous banquet, and parties and banquets are the high spots of our lives too. Christ invites us now to a banquet. We are to feed at his table and receive at the same time a promise of living forever with him. With this food we draw life from him, draw on his energy and vitality.

● We cannot go on living the old kind of life. With Christ living in us, can we continue being disagreeable, touchy, standing on our rights? By going outside of ourselves and our own interests, putting the needs and happiness of others first, we imitate Christ, and, learning in this way to know him, we begin to have some foretaste of the joy which will be ours when united to him forever.

GENERAL INTERCESSIONS:

Introduction: Eating of the Eucharist means far more than performing a momentary act of piety or devotion. To taste of the Lord's Supper is to taste a whole new way of life; it is to taste of the very wisdom and love that will transform the world. Let us pray for such transformed lives, as we respond: **LORD, GIVE US ETERNAL LIFE.**

1. That the Living Bread of Christ may unite the Church in a brotherhood of charity and service, we pray to the Lord.

2. That those who hunger for a deeper significance to life may find it in the joy and thanksgiving of Christians, we . . .

3. That Christians may offer the world the power and wisdom of the Gospel, rather than the human wisdom which grasps for power, we . . .

4. That, as we taste the Lord's goodness in this Eucharist, we may prepare ourselves for an altogether new way of living, we . . .

5. For persons whom we have scandalized by our failure to live according to the justice and peace of Christ, we . . .

*(Additional invocations)*_____

Conclusion: All glory be yours, Father, for the life and wisdom you have revealed in Jesus Christ. May we who now prepare to join in his sacrifice be filled with a spirit of praise and thanksgiving, so that our lives may become the sign of your love in and for the world. We make our prayer through the same Christ our Lord.

ADDITIONAL INVITATION TO COMMUNION:

Behold the Living Bread of everlasting life!

PRAYER AFTER COMMUNION:

"Anyone who eats this bread will love forever." Confident of Christ's promise, let us pray that our whole lives may become a "eucharist," an act of praise and thanksgiving to the Father.

Twenty-first Sunday of the Year

THEME: FAITHFULNESS

INTRODUCTION:
Faithfulness is usually understood as a human project, as the consistent choice to live by the values we consider true and important. But for a Christian such fidelity is rooted less in human decision than in God's choice to communicate himself to the world through Jesus Christ. God believed enough in human beings to make them members of his Son's body. Our fidelity to each other, in mutual trust and love, is thus a reflection of God's own faithfulness to men.

INVITATION TO PENITENTIAL RITE:
Sometimes we forget that the greatest proof of our love for another consists in our choice to stand by that person in good times and bad. With this in mind, let us honestly examine ourselves on the virtue of faithfulness.

FORM C: *(Optional invocations)*
Faithful to your word, you love us even though we sin: Lord, have mercy.

Faithful to your Father's will, you cleanse us by your own blood: Christ . . .

Faithful to your promise, you send us the Spirit of Truth: Lord . . .

OPENING PRAYER:
Let us pray for faithfulness and integrity in our relations with God and with one another.

READINGS:
1) **Jos. 24:1-2, 15-17, 18.** Periodically the Israelites celebrated God's faithfulness to them through a ceremony of covenant-renewal. Today's passage from Joshua describes how the people rededicated themselves to serve the Lord alone at such a covenant ceremony.

2) **Eph. 5:21-32.** The faithful love between husband and wife expresses, in Paul's mind, the intimate relation between Christ and the Church which is his body.

3) **Jn. 6:60-69.** Today we conclude the reading of the sixth chapter of John's Gospel, which has told of Christ as the Bread of Life. As Jesus remarks, the words he has spoken are "spirit and life" for the believer.

HOMILY NOTES:
• Israel was unfaithful to God on many occasions. But God con-

tinued to renew his invitations and offer his protection. Israel renewed her promise to honor God faithfully, as she had solemnly agreed in the Covenant that had been made.

● But we cannot afford to be smug about this backsliding; it is not peculiar to Israel. We have much less excuse for our infidelity. Christ, who came to establish the New Covenant, pointed to disunity and underlined the destruction that results. But that most familiar and intimate of relationships, of covenants, that of marriage, is one that Paul points to as a pattern for Christ's love of his Church.

● Fidelity demands difficult things of us, but we must try to accept them, overcome the stumbling blocks as Peter tried valiantly to do in the face of skeptics who could not take the strange and challenging claims of Christ.

GENERAL INTERCESSIONS:

Invitation: Paul reminds us, in today's second reading, that we are the living parts of Christ's body. Since we draw our life of faith only in and through Christ, let us petition him for our deepest needs, as we respond: **LORD, YOU HAVE THE WORDS OF LIFE.**

1. That the Church may faithfully adhere to Christ, who sacrificed himself to make her holy, we pray to the Lord.

2. That we may, at this Eucharist, renew our baptismal promises to live totally for Christ and for the members of his body, we . . .

3. That married couples may find, in their love and fidelity toward each other, a sign of that selfless love Christ has for his Church, we . . .

4. That men who live in misery and hopelessness may have their burden lightened through Christ's message of everlasting life, we . . .

5. For biblical scholars who work to open the treasures of God's Word to ever-increasing numbers of people, we . . .

*(Additional invocations)*_____

Conclusion: Father, keep us ever faithful to your word, for it is truly a light in our darkness. Open our hearts to the life you offer day by day; keep us steady when we feel confused, comfort us when we feel hurt and depressed, and lead us to the peace only you can give, through Christ our Lord.

ADDITIONAL INVITATION TO COMMUNION:
Behold Christ, who loved the Church and sacrificed himself for her!

PRAYER AFTER COMMUNION:
Peter confessed, in the Gospel passage for today, "Lord, whom shall we go to? You have the message of eternal life, and we believe." Let us pray, giving thanks that God has granted us, in Christ, a faith which can make every day a new beginning.

Twenty-second
Sunday of the Year

THEME: KEEPING THE LAW

INTRODUCTION:

When someone becomes so involved with details that he misses the real point of a topic under discussion, we often remark, "He can't see the forest for the trees." The same sort of blindness can afflict persons in the life of faith. The authentic purpose of religious laws is to unify the community of believers in charity and peace. When that purpose is lost sight of, it is time to listen once more to Jesus' warning in today's Gospel: "You put aside the commandment of God to cling to human traditions."

INVITATION TO PENITENTIAL RITE:

History is full of atrocities committed in the name of piety and religious law. As we prepare for the Eucharist, let us take a hard look at those times we may have used religious practice as an excuse to perpetuate barriers of intolerance and misunderstanding.

FORM C: *(Optional invocations)*

Source of goodness, Fountain of blessing: Lord, have mercy.
Light of the world, bringer of peace: Christ . . .
Love of the Father, brother of men: Lord . . .

OPENING PRAYER:

Let us pray that, as we listen to God's word, his truth may dwell in our hearts through faith.

READINGS:

1) **Dt. 4:1-2, 6-8.** In the best tradition of the Old Testament, God's law was a sign of his close relation to his people through the covenant. Our passage from Deuteronomy reflects this tradition; religious laws and customs were given so that Israel might have life.

2) **Jas. 1:17-18, 21-22, 27.** St. James declares that God's word will same us only if, after hearing it, we act upon its impulse toward loving service.

3) **Mk. 7:1-8, 14-15, 21-23.** Today's Gospel shows that Jesus' complaint against the Pharisees was twofold: they substituted human regulations for the real commands of God, and they valued pious display more than sincerity of heart.

HOMILY NOTES:

- In a mistaken idea of serving God more fully the Scribes had added innumerable extra details to the Law. For they felt that they were serving God perfectly in keeping these minute observances.
- We miss the point unless we realize that the Pharisees were thought to be the best people, the utterly faithful in devotion to God. What had gone wrong in them was a universal, human thing — a desire to find security in structures and achievements added to self-righteousness.
- Christ's words to the Pharisees are a challenge to us and we can hardly deny that they apply to us. Catholic people have been oblivious to many of the real human needs around them, the lonely, the fatherless, the widowed. We have failed to build up a true Christian community.

GENERAL INTERCESSIONS:

Invitation: For a Christian there is no higher law than the Gospel command to love God above all things and our neighbor as ourselves. Let us pray for fidelity to this law of charity, as we respond: **LORD, DIRECT OUR HEARTS.**

1. That the Church may always be renewed and purified by the word of Christ's Gospel, we pray to the Lord.

2. That we may bring hope to the despairing more through loving action than through pious words, we . . .

3. That our hearts may be filled with the honest desire to live for one another, so that we may worship in spirit and in truth, we . . .

4. That the Father may protect all those who are traveling on our highways today, we . . .

5. That the sick and the dying may be comforted by the Father of all light and mercy, we . . .

*(Additional invocations)*_____

Conclusion: Father, you are the source of all light, all consolation, and all charity. Direct our hearts in the paths of justice and mercy, and assist us in obeying the Gospel command of love this day and every day of our lives, through Christ our Lord.

ADDITIONAL INVITATION TO COMMUNION:
Behold Christ, the Father's perfect gift to men!

PRAYER AFTER COMMUNION:
James issued a stern warning to Christians in today's second reading: "Do what the word tells you, and not just listen to it and deceive yourselves." Let us pray for hearts that not only hear and accept the Gospel, but seek for new ways to apply it to daily living.

Twenty-third Sunday of the Year

THEME: THE EYES OF FAITH

INTRODUCTION:

Faith is both a new kind of understanding and a new way of seeing things. For example, an ancient Egyptian might have looked at Israel's exodus as simply the unfortunate escape of some slaves. But the faith of Moses and the Hebrew people saw in the same event a sign of God's saving power. Similarly, Jesus' work of healing the blind and the deaf can only be seen by faith. These cures are the sign that God's kingdom is breaking in upon men, that the world has been fundamentally changed and given a new direction. Through the eyes of faith we see in Christ the beginning of a new life and a new hope for the world.

INVITATION TO PENITENTIAL RITE:

It is commonly said that people hear only what they want to hear, and see only what they want to see. Have we, perhaps, been closing our eyes to the presence and action of Christ right in our very midst? Let us ponder this question, as we prepare to celebrate the Eucharist.

FORM C: *(Optional invocations)*

You speak to us in Word and Sacrament: Lord, have mercy.

You are present to heal and forgive us: Christ . . .

You reveal yourself in your mercy to the poor and the neglected: Lord . . .

OPENING PRAYER:

Let us pray that the poverty of our faith may be enriched by the mercy of the Father who saves us in Christ.

READINGS:

1) **Is. 35:4-7.** Isaiah's hopeful message was addressed to a nation that experienced the crushing bitterness of exile. But even the blind, the deaf, and the lame will dance and rejoice at the approach of God's salvation.

2) **Jas. 2:1-5.** St. James remarks that the poor of this world are often those chosen by God to be rich in faith and heirs of Christ's Kingdom.

3) **Mk. 7:31-37.** In our first reading from Isaiah, the healing of the blind and the deaf was a sign of future deliverance by God's power. Mark's Gospel shows that Jesus' work of healing means the reign of God has now taken hold of the world at its root.

HOMILY NOTES:

• In the early Church, Baptism was called "enlightenment." As

114

Christians, we live by the truth God has revealed; we are no longer in darkness, but have the light of Christ. We must share this with others.

● Faith does not mean seeing clearly and knowing the answers. It means trusting God amid doubt and uncertainty; being open to truth as far as we can discern it in God's word in Scripture, in the reality of our lives. Prejudice and fear can deafen and blind us to the truth. We can look for a place to hide away from insecurity and uncertainty. The prophets announced that at Christ's coming "the eyes of the blind would be opened."

● The times foretold have come; Christ's miracles are not just acts of compassion or displays of power but signs that man can be freed from the evil inherent in this world. Christ uses water and oil in the sacraments to heal us. With open eyes and unstopped ears we can discern the signs of the Kingdom.

GENERAL INTERCESSIONS:

Invitation: People without spiritual vision are usually people without hope, because they fail to see the possibility of meaningful change in their lives. Let us pray for a clearer vision of faith and a firmer purpose to live the Gospel, as we respond: **LORD, HELP US TO SEE.**

1. That the Church may serve as a sacrament of healing to bind up the wounds and divisions of men in our world, we pray to the Lord.

2. That men who face the grim realities of bloodshed and war may discover the vision of a just and lasting peace, we . . .

3. That the physically handicapped, especially the deaf, the mute, and the blind, may find new ways to lead productive and happy lives, we . . .

4. That persons exiled from their homes and their native countries may find a joyful welcome in the homes of Christians, we . . .

5. That the hearts of people who have closed their eyes to the squalor, pain, and poverty around them may be opened by God's mercy, we . . .

*(Additional invocations)*_____

Conclusion: God and Father of our Lord Jesus Christ, no one who seeks your mercy in faith will ever be disappointed. We ask you, open our eyes and our ears to the presence of your kingdom in our work, our world and our worship, through Christ our Lord.

ADDITIONAL INVITATION TO COMMUNION:
Behold the Lord who makes the deaf hear and the blind see!

PRAYER AFTER COMMUNION:
"It is the Lord who gives sight to the blind, who raises up those who are bowed down." Let us pray that all of us who have eaten at this table may be given a new vision of the meaning of Christ's Gospel for our lives.

Twenty-fourth Sunday of the Year

THEME: THE CROSS

INTRODUCTION:
Few elements in the Christian message are so critical, yet so often misunderstood, as the cross of Jesus. The cross is not an invitation to lead a miserable, dehumanizing life; it is rather a call to hope in the face of those sufferings which are the normal accompaniments of human existence. As Cardinal Newman once put it, the cross is the measure of the world; it calls all human values into question by revealing a love forceful enough to bridge the terrifying gap between death and life.

INVITATION TO PENITENTIAL RITE:
Christianity is more than a religion of personal fulfillment: it has important social implications as well. St. James will reaffirm this point in today's second reading: belief without action is simply dead faith. As we prepare ourselves for worship, let us examine ourselves on the quality and depth of our faith-in-action.

FORM C: *(Optional invocations)*
We praise your cross as the source of life and forgiveness: Lord, have mercy.
We rejoice in your power to save us from the sting of death: Christ...
We confess that you are the Christ, Son of the living God: Lord . . .

OPENING PRAYER:
Let us pray for a mature spirit of discipleship, for the willingness to risk losing our lives in order to find them again in Christ.

READINGS:
1) **Is. 50:5-9.** Four times in the prophet Isaiah we hear descriptions of a mysterious "servant of the Lord," who, by his fidelity, will bring salvation to the people. Together these four passages are called the "servant songs," and today we hear the third one of them. The early Church saw in Jesus the perfect "servant of the Lord" who brings salvation through his cross and suffering.
2) **Jas. 2:14-18.** To believe, St. James tells us, means nothing if it is not expressed in charitable action for the sake of others.
3) **Mk. 8:27-35.** Throughout the early chapters of Mark's Gospel there is a progressive revelation of who Jesus is and what his destiny must be. Today we hear Jesus identify himself with the suffering servant described by the prophet Isaiah.

HOMILY NOTES:

● Our human situation is one in which we are inevitably caught up in a world-gone-wrong. Sooner or later we are involved in suffering; we still have to face death.

● Through our Lord's passion and death he has provided us with a way through to the fullness of life that we long for. Christ has done this, not by avoiding suffering and death but by facing them, accepting them willingly out of love for us, and in doing so he was glorified by his Father.

● Christ has given meaning to all human suffering and death. They are still mysterious, but now they can be an expression of our love, the way through to human fulfillment. The cross is a sign of hope and life for each of us.

GENERAL INTERCESSIONS:

Invitation: As a people called not only to hear and believe the word of the Gospel, but also to act vigorously upon it, let us offer prayer for the needs of God's world and his Church. Our response is: **IN YOUR GOODNESS, LORD, HEAR US.**

1. That the Church may live and serve in the world as a sign of hope for all who suffer, we pray to the Lord.

2. That people who have never known anything but misery and hardship may find peace and comfort in the charity of Christians we . . .

3. That the faith of Christians may grow strong in the truth and active in deeds of compassion, we . . .

4. That we may see, in this celebration of the death and resurrection of Jesus, a sign of our call to total conversion of life, we . . .

*(Additional invocations)*_____

Conclusion: Father, we praise you for showing us the way to life through the cross of Jesus, your Son. May we have the courage to take up that cross daily, and to discover what our lives really mean by pouring them out in love for one another, through the same Jesus Christ our Lord.

ADDITIONAL INVITATION TO COMMUNION:

Behold Christ, whose cross is life and salvation!

PRAYER AFTER COMMUNION:

"If anyone wants to be a follower of mine, let him renounce himself and take up his cross and follow me." Let us pray, reaffirming our decision to live a Christianity that risks losing everything for the sake of the Gospel.

Twenty-fifth Sunday of the Year

THEME: HUMBLE SERVICE

INTRODUCTION:
In the normal conduct of human affairs, power and publicity command wide respect. When Christ came, he challenged this notion by living in a condition of weakness among the poor and downtrodden. Through a life of humble service Jesus revealed the sources of real power among men: gentleness and the constant search for peace. We can share this power of Christ only if we are willing to serve one another in humility and truth.

INVITATION TO PENITENTIAL RITE:
As Christians, my friends, we are called to be peacemakers, full of compassion and tireless in doing good. Failure to live in this way makes the name of Christian little more than a sham and an hypocrisy. Let us examine our hearts, asking ourselves if we are truly peacemakers in the name of Christ.

FORM C: *(Optional invocations)*
Though you were rich, you became poor as the servant of all: Lord, have mercy.

Though you were the Father's Word and Wisdom, you revealed yourself in weakness: Christ . . .

Though you were crucified, you were proclaimed Son of God in power: Lord . . .

OPENING PRAYER:
Let us pray that the Lord who is in our midst will make of us his humble servants.

READINGS:
1) **Wis. 2:12, 17-20.** The virtuous man is a sign of contradiction — not by his severity, but by his gentleness. The Book of Wisdom describes such a man, tortured and condemned by his enemies, but declared just by the wisdom of God.

2) **Jas. 3:16—4:3.** St. James informs us that the wisdom of God is manifested by men who are peacemakers. Persons who have deep peace in their hearts will be known by the virtues of kindness and humility.

3) **Mk. 9:30-37.** Last Sunday, Jesus revealed to the disciples his mission as suffering servant of the Lord. Today, Mark's Gospel describes Jesus as the gentle servant whose death will result in life for all.

HOMILY NOTES:
● By his life and actions, Christ has turned our values upside down.

He has shown us that true greatness is not a matter of power and respectability, but is to be found only in the service of others.

● "The Son of Man came not to be served but to serve, and to give his life as a ransom for many." He became our servant so that we might share his glory. He gave himself completely, to the extent of dying for us. This was the ultimate test of his love.

● If we call ourselves Christians, we too must live a life of service, not seeking any reward. It is easy enough to give when we feel in a generous mood. It is hard to be always willing to serve when this means constant drudgery or when we meet with ingratitude.

● Perhaps we will be encouraged if we remember that Christ is with us in our service, giving his love to others through us. If we are asked to share his cross, we can be sure that we will also share in his resurrection.

GENERAL INTERCESSIONS:

Invitation: St. Augustine once told his people that love praises the Lord, while discord is a blasphemy. We heard much the same view in our reading from the apostle James, who labeled jealousy, disharmony, and ambition as sins against God's wisdom. Let us pray now for the peace and harmony of the world, as we respond: **LORD, UNITE US IN PEACE.**

1. That peace may dwell in the hearts of men, binding them in a brotherhood of mutual service, we pray to the Lord.

2. That nations committed to programs of violence and destruction may be converted to the way of peace, we . . .

3. That through our worship in Word and sacrament we may be united to the suffering of Jesus, so as to share his glory, we . . .

4. For those who face the daily cruelty of hunger and thirst, we . . .

5. For prisoners of war, for persons imprisoned by fear, and for men who have never heard the Good News of Christ, we . . .

(Additional invocations) _____

Conclusion: Raise up among us, Father, true prophets of your peace. Guide us into the ways of humble service so that we who claim the name of Christian may become the heralds of your love in a world where charity threatens to grow cold. We ask you to grant this and every petition through Christ our Lord.

ADDITIONAL INVITATION TO COMMUNION:
Behold the Son of Man, crucified in weakness and raised up in glory!

PRAYER AFTER COMMUNION:
In the psalm following the first reading we prayed: "I have God for my help; the Lord upholds my life." Let us pray that, as we have eaten and drunk with Christ in this sacrament, we may serve him humbly in one another.

Twenty-sixth Sunday of the Year

THEME: THE HOLY SPIRIT IN US

INTRODUCTION:
Men have always been tempted to create gods in their own image — gods that can easily be manipulated, controlled, and restricted. Today's readings reveal that the Spirit of the living God cannot be confined by human efforts. The Spirit works in the most extraordinary persons and events, and it is our task to discover, through prayer and fidelity to the Gospel, where and when the Spirit is calling us.

INVITATION TO PENITENTIAL RITE:
Brothers and sisters, do we really believe that the Spirit who raised Jesus from death is also at work among us, even in the most humble circumstances of our lives? Let us pause to consider whether we have tried to restrict the working of the Spirit only to those moments when we feel pious and comfortable.

FORM C: *(Optional invocations)*
When we do not know how to pray, your Spirit prays in us: Lord, have mercy.

When we are wretched and afflicted, your Spirit brings consolation: Christ . . .

When our sins tempt us to despair, your Spirit raises us up in hope: Lord . . .

OPENING PRAYER:
Let us pray that our eyes may be open to the presence of God's Spirit, especially among those whom the world despises as poor and contemptible.

READINGS:
1) **Nm. 11:25-29.** Our first reading from the Book of Numbers is closely related to today's Gospel. Both readings show the Spirit of God at work among people we are tempted to consider unlikely and unworthy.

2) **Jas. 5:1-6.** St. James uses extremely strong language as a warning against rich people who are stingy about giving to the poor. Wealth, if kept for selfish purposes, corrodes the life of the Spirit in us.

3) **Mk. 9:38-43, 45, 47-48.** In Mark's Gospel Jesus tells his disciples that whoever is not against him is for him. We are reminded of the first reading, which reveals the Spirit at work beyond the confines of established religion.

HOMILY NOTES:
• The Spirit of God can possess any man and speak through him.

God will not always choose those in authority, the learned, the respectable, or even acknowledged Christians, to make his will known.

● The two readings show us that, even outside the official body of the Church, men are moved by the Spirit. In each case we are told firmly to acknowledge the Spirit in them. We have assumed that only the Church's official declarations can contain truth, and have closed our ears to its coming from unacceptable sources even within that Church, with the result that we have become rigid, closed, authoritarian, and smug. Also, it might be said that we have kept our riches to ourselves.

● Now, in time of difficulty, we take out warm garments and find them full of moths. Other Christian traditions have often kept closer to true Christianity, have shown more concern for the poor, the lonely, the widowed. Jesus urges us to take radical measures to prevent our becoming selfish. We have acted as if only we were the salt of life. If we lose our power to season, of what use are we?

GENERAL INTERCESSIONS:

Invitation: The Spirit of Jesus prays in us, even when we fell unable to make petition to the Father. Relying on the strength of that Spirit poured into our hearts by faith, let us pray: **YOUR WORD, LORD, IS SPIRIT AND LIFE.**

1. That the Spirit of Jesus may give the Church courage to proclaim the Gospel even in the face of opposition and hostility, we pray to the Lord.

2. That God may raise up in his Church prophets of wisdom and compassionate understanding, we . . .

3. That wealthy men and nations may use their means to relieve the suffering of the poor, we . . .

4. That under the guidance of the Spirit, Christians may develop a deeper love and understanding of the wisdom of God in Scripture, we . . .

*(Additional invocations)*_____

Conclusion: Father, may you be blessed and praised by every creature. May the presence of your Spirit flood our lives with mercy and compassion, so that all men may come to know you, the true and living God, and him whom you sent and through whom we make this prayer: Jesus Christ our Lord.

ADDITIONAL INVITATION TO COMMUNION:

Behold Jesus, the Lord of creation and giver of the Spirit!

PRAYER AFTER COMMUNION:

The Lord, in his Gospel, told us: "If anyone gives you a cup of water to drink just because you belong to Christ . . . he will certainly not lose his reward." Let us pray for the insight to see God's Spirit working even in the most surprising persons and events of our time.

Twenty-seventh Sunday of the Year

THEME: COMMUNITY

INTRODUCTION:

No man can develop the full potential of his human and Christian personality in total isolation from others. From the beginning man was created for the companionship of marriage and for the brotherhood of faith in Jesus. Today's Mass affords us the opportunity to see that, apart from the love of others, life becomes stifled and meaningless.

INVITATION TO PENITENTIAL RITE:

Dear friends, God's plan through history has been to draw men gradually into deeper communion with one another. Starting with the basic union between man and wife in marriage, the Lord has united all men now as brothers of Jesus. Let us take a moment to consider how we have resisted God's call to a deeper fellowship in love and faith.

FORM C: *(Optional invocations)*

You created men to live in love and not in loneliness: Lord, have mercy.

You brought us together as brothers through the cross: Christ . . .

You promised the Kingdom to those with the simple faith of children: Lord . . .

OPENING PRAYER:

Let us pray that Christ will, in his love for men, break down the barriers that separate and divide us from one another.

READINGS:

1) **Gn. 2:18-24.** The opening chapters of Genesis are a meditation on God's creative power and his plan for human community. The opening words of today's reading establish the basic theme of the entire Bible: "It is not good for man to be alone."

2) **Heb. 2:9-11.** We who were sanctified in the blood of Jesus have become his brothers; we share his own community relation with Father and Holy Spirit.

3) **Mk. 10:2-16.** The Christian ideal of a permanent bond of love in marriage is based on Jesus' teaching that the union between husband and wife reflects God's own fidelity to his promises. We hear that ideal expressed in our reading from Mark's Gospel.

HOMILY NOTES:

• We recognize in Scripture the value placed on companionship, community and married love. Man develops and grows in association, in contact with others. When he is accepted in a community, an attitude of confidence and closeness develops.

● In the community of the family he becomes a caring, unselfish and serving person, a loyal partner to his wife. In the wider community he enriches the group by his presence and contribution, and puts himself at the service of his fellows.

● Children do not count for less in the community; they are an integral part of it and each is important as an individual. We all have a duty — man, woman and child — to build and preserve the spirit of community at home, at work or at leisure.

● Christ separated himself from the Godhead and took our humanity. His work on earth made it possible for us to enter into his Kingdom, a heavenly community. Christ has given us a way of love, service and self-sacrifice which leads to this Kingdom.

GENERAL INTERCESSIONS:

Invitation: The very life of God is based on the principle of community: Father, Son and Holy Spirit dwell in a union so intense that it bursts into our own lives, filling them with color, vision, and enthusiasm. Let us pray for a fuller communion with God and among ourselves, as we respond: **LORD, UNITE US IN FAITH.**

1. That our fellowship in God's Church may draw all men toward the unity for which Jesus prayed before his death, we pray to the Lord.

2. That husbands and wives may find new cause for joy in marriage through their common faith in Christ, we . . .

3. That Christians may cooperate with all men of good will who seek a world united in peace, we . . .

4. That parents may love their children tenderly, since it is to such as these that God's Kingdom belongs, we . . .

5. For those isolated from human companionship in prisons and mental hospitals, we . . .

(Additional invocations) _____

Conclusion: Father, we thank you for sharing your life among us in word, in bread, in the joy of one another. May our communion in your life bring us, rejoicing, into the Kingdom of your glory, through Christ our Lord.

ADDITIONAL INVITATION TO COMMUNION:
Behold our brother Jesus, crowned with glory and splendor!

PRAYER AFTER COMMUNION:
"Let the little children come to me . . . for it is to such as these that the Kingdom of God belongs." Beloved in Christ, let us pray for the openness to receive God's Kingdom with the simplicity of children.

123

Twenty-eighth Sunday of the Year

THEME: WISDOM, THE WORD OF GOD

INTRODUCTION:

To the average man God's Wisdom will regularly appear as foolishness. In fact, when we hear Jesus telling a rich young man to forfeit his wealth, we are tempted to think of religious fanaticism or economic naiveté. But the hard fact is that, if a Christian is serious about his commitment in faith, he must be willing to make sacrifices that would astonish the worldly-wise.

INVITATION TO PENITENTIAL RITE:

Sometimes, on hearing the uncomfortable words of the Gospel, we are inclined to say: "All of that is very noble, but it doesn't apply to me." Do we ever consider that God's word is not addressed to men in general, but to *me specifically*? Let us ponder on this for a moment in our hearts.

FORM C: *(Optional invocations)*

Wisdom greater than wealth or beauty: Lord, have mercy.
Word of God alive and active: Christ . . .
Faithful witness, messenger of salvation: Lord . . .

OPENING PRAYER:

Let us pray, brothers and sisters, for the wisdom and understanding which are the gifts of Jesus' Spirit in us.

READINGS:

1) **Wis. 7:7-11.** Our first reading is a prayer for that wisdom which is the very radiance of God's glory. The themes of this passage seem to have influenced the author of the Letter to the Hebrews from which our second reading will be taken.
2) **Heb. 4:12-13.** A hymn to the living, the active Word of God constitutes the second reading for today's liturgy.
3) **Mk. 10:17-30.** Mark's story of the encounter between Jesus and the rich young man is a classic statement of the degree to which Christians are expected to follow the Lord. Nothing less than total dedication is worthy of the Christian Gospel.

HOMILY NOTES:

● For the Jews wisdom was not abstract philosophy, but something vital, a driving force. They described wisdom in vigorous personal terms.

- With the coming of Christ, Wisdom, the Word of God, revealed himself as a Person, the Word who is life; the Word, as John says, "that we have heard, that we have seen with our eyes, that we have touched with our hands."
- To witness to this God-made-man is not just to talk about him but to present him directly. "I live now, no, Christ lives in me." Such identification necessarily involves suffering and persecution.
- To follow Christ requires a radical rethinking of our lives. It is not enough, as Jesus tells the rich young man, to observe the commandments. A total generosity is needed, giving all that one has.
- The Word of God is alive and active; no created thing can hide from him, everything is open to the eyes of the one to whom we must give an account of ourselves.

GENERAL INTERCESSIONS:

Invitation: The Scriptures are given a place of honor in our churches; but, to be effective, the Word of God must catch fire in our own minds and hearts. Let us pray for the grace to meet Christ as fully in the Bible as we do in the Eucharist. Our response is: **LORD, YOUR WORD IS OUR LIFE.**

1. That the Scriptures may become for us a vital challenge to our usual ways of thinking and living, we pray to the Lord.

2. That the Word and Wisdom of God may purify our hearts and lead us to value God's Kingdom above personal ambitions for wealth and success, we . . .

3. That those committed to the instruction and catechesis of others in the faith of Christ may receive our cooperation and support, we . . .

4. That students may grow in the love of wisdom both human and divine, we . . .

5. For persons unable or unwilling to hear the Word of God in faith and love, we . . .

(Additional invocations) _____

Conclusion: Lord Jesus Christ, Word and Wisdom of the Father, we pray for a clearer awareness of your presence among us. As we prepare to eat and drink of your supper, hear these petitions and answer them in your mercy. We ask this of you who live and reign with the Father and the Holy Spirit, now and forever.

ADDITIONAL INVITATION TO COMMUNION:

Behold Christ, Wisdom of the Father and radiance of his glory!

PRAYER AFTER COMMUNION:

"I prayed and understanding was given me; I entreated, and the spirit of Wisdom came to me." Let us pray in our hearts, with thanksgiving, for the wisdom of Christ, which renews our lives day by day.

Twenty-ninth Sunday of the Year

THEME: CHRIST THE SERVANT

INTRODUCTION:
It may be fairly easy to feel an attraction for Christ as a pleasant, affable idealist. But we may balk at the image of Christ as a servant — a suffering, crucified servant at that. For the Christian message offers more than milk and honey; it offers a strong meat and a heady wine. Do we have the couage to accept the lordship of a Christ who declared that persons who want to be first should start by becoming last?

INVITATION TO PENITENTIAL RITE:
My brothers and sisters, we have in Jesus a brother who knew the full extent of human weakness and temptation. Let us call to mind our sins, confident that Jesus, our high priest, has won the Father's mercy for men.

FORM C: *(Optional invocations)*
You were weak and tempted as we are: Lord, have mercy.
You were the humble servant of all: Christ . . .
You were crushed by suffering but raised in glory: Lord . . .

OPENING PRAYER:
Let us pray that, as we were baptized into the death of Jesus, we may live his risen life through grace.

READINGS:
1) **Is. 53:10-11.** A few weeks ago we heard the third "servant song" of the prophet Isaiah. Today we hear the fourth and final one of these songs, which describes the way in which God saves his just servant, who has been crushed by suffering.
2) **Heb. 4:14-16.** The Letter to the Hebrews was probably written to bring encouragement to an early community of frightened and vacillating Christians. The author affirms that Christians can, with confidence, depend on the mercy of God, since in Jesus we have a high priest fully acquainted with our weakness.
3) **Mk. 10:35-45.** Jesus remarks, in today's Gospel passage, that the only way to be first in the Father's sight is to become the humblest servant of all.

HOMILY NOTES:
● Christ means us to share with him in his glory, but he says to us what he said to James and John, "Can you drink the cup that I shall drink? Can you go the whole way with me in doing the will of my Father?"

- He came on earth to do the will of his Father, not to have his own way. He taught and healed, denounced injustice and indifference, and exposed false religion. In doing this he provoked misunderstanding and antagonism, persecution and death. But, cost what it might, he would do his Father's will.
- God's will for us is clear. Like Christ, we must care for those in trouble and work to eliminate injustice. Nobody likes extra work; we all want to be comfortable and to have our own way. It calls for courage to face up to our Christian responsibility.
- But, as we are reminded in the Epistle, Jesus feels for us in our weakness because he has shared it. He will help us to be a servant as he was, and as we must be.

GENERAL INTERCESSIONS:
Invitation: Since by his death and rising Christ has given us the chance to begin our lives again, we can speak to the Father without fear and without shame. Let us open our hearts in complete confidence, as we pray: **MAY YOUR LOVE BE WITH US, LORD.**
1. That the faith of the Church may become for the world the unfailing sign of God's ability to bring life out of death and hope out of despair, we pray to the Lord.
2. That leaders of churches and civil governments may exercise the kind of authority that results from humble, generous service, we . . .
3. That the sacrifice of Jesus may give persons who are "down and out" the courage to pick up the fragments of their lives and begin again, we . . .
4. For persons who are dying of starvation and malnutrition, we . . .
5. For men who are struggling to free themselves from addiction to drugs, we . . .

*(Additional invocations)*_____

Conclusion: Father, we come into your presence, conscious of our weakness but confident of your power to save. May your unfailing love give us strength to be servants of the truth, even when this demands drinking the cup of Jesus' passion. We make our prayer through the same Christ our Lord.

ADDITIONAL INVITATION TO COMMUNION:
Behold Jesus, the high priest who shared our weakness!

PRAYER AFTER COMMUNION:
"Anyone who wants to become great among you must be your servant, and anyone who wants to be first among you must be slave to all." Let us pray, uniting ourselves to Jesus in his servantship, and promising to live as a people dedicated to the humility that brings greatness in God's sight.

Thirtieth Sunday of the Year

THEME: RETURN FROM EXILE

INTRODUCTION:
The Bible might well be subtitled: "A Handbook for People on Their Way Home Again." For the Scriptures record the meandering history of individuals and nations trying to find their way back to the God and Father who gave them life. It is the story of exiles returning home, of estranged sinners restored to peace, of blind men given back their sight. The Bible is the personal biography of all of us; it is the story of our return, bloody and stumbling, to the Father who loved us even when we were a long way from home.

INVITATION TO PENITENTIAL RITE:
Our second reading for today will explain that Christ "can sympathize with those who are ignorant or uncertain because he too lives in the limitations of weakness." Let us seek forgiveness for the times we have had no patience or sympathy with the weaknesses of persons with whom we live and work.

FORM C: *(Optional invocations)*
Sharing the limits of our weakness, you offered your life in sacrifice: Lord, have mercy.
Preaching the Good News of peace, you brought sight to the blind: Christ . . .
Rising in glory, you became the true and everlasting priest: Lord . . .

OPENING PRAYER:
Let us pray, longing for that time when every tear will be wiped away, and we will find ourselves at home with the Father.

READINGS:
1) **Jer. 31:7-9.** The prophet Jeremiah looked toward a time when Israel would return from the misery of exile. On that day of salvation, Jeremiah declared, the blind, the lame, and the tearful would find comfort in a fatherly God.

2) **Heb. 5:1-6.** Our second reading, from the Letter to the Hebrews, meditates on the priesthood of Jesus. Because our Lord shared the human condition so totally, he is in a position to sympathize with our own feelings of weakness and inadequacy.

3) **Mk. 10:46-52.** Jesus' restoration of sight to the blind man is a sign of our own restoration to vision and happiness through faith and the waters of Baptism.

128

HOMILY NOTES:
- We often do not appreciate what we have until we lose it. We do not appreciate home and country until exiled, as the Israelites were.
- Punished for their idolatry, they at last learned that theirs was a true and loving God, loving them in their unfaithfulness. He would lead them back home and not remember their sins. Likewise, the blind man of Jericho had been given his sight, and, therefore, knew his loss. He begged for the gift of sight again.
- We are returned exiles also, blind men with sight restored. Through our Baptism we are brought home to the house of our Father, have our eyes opened to the light of his truth. This is accomplished for us by Christ, who, although he was God's Son, suffered and died for us, so that he might be raised up and bring us with him to the Father.
- We are now at home, and can confidently approach our Father who loves and provides for us.

GENERAL INTERCESSIONS:
Invitation: It is possible to live comfortably and work successfully, yet all the time remain estranged from the deepest meaning of life. We need the constant effort of prayer to bring us back to our Christian roots, to help our hearts return to the Father who has called us sons in Jesus. Let us pray, then, as we respond: **LORD, BRING US BACK TO YOU.**

1. That our liberation from sin through Baptism and Penance may keep our hearts firm in the ways of God's truth, we pray to the Lord.
2. That all of us who have died and risen with Christ may follow him back to the Father, who is the fountain of life and happiness, we . . .
3. That the broken-hearted may be given a new lease on life through the mercy of Christ, who shared our weakness, we . . .
4. For blind persons who have never seen the color and beauty of creation, we . . .

*(Additional invocations)*_____

Conclusion: Father, wipe away our tears and bring us back home to you. Restore us by your love, for we believe that you have the power to return to blind men their sight and to broken men their courage. We make our prayer through Christ our Lord.

ADDITIONAL INVITATION TO COMMUNION:
Behold the Lord who gives sight to the blind!

PRAYER AFTER COMMUNION:
The blind man of today's Gospel cried out: "Son of David, Jesus, have pity on me." Filled with the light of Christ's presence, let us pray that we may communicate his mercy to all those who need the loving concern of a friend.

Thirty-first Sunday of the Year

THEME: LAW AND ORDER

INTRODUCTION:
For many Americans "law and order" has become largely a political slogan. That can be unfortunate, because it may prevent our seeing the deeper meaning of law in the context of the Gospel. The real purpose of law is to insure the cohesion and continuity of a social body. For Christians the only law which can provide such insurance is Jesus' command to love both God and neighbor with every ounce of our understanding and strength.

INVITATION TO PENITENTIAL RITE:
Sometimes in looking for the one "great moment" to show our love for God and neighbor, we miss the thousand little opportunities. Can we really say that our love for one another is as daily as bread? If not, it is time to begin trying again.

FORM C: *(Optional invocations)*
You taught us that mercy is more important than sacrifice: Lord, have mercy.
You have taken away our hearts of stone and given us new hearts to know and love you: Christ . . .
You remain forever living to intercede for all who journey to the Father: Lord . . .

OPENING PRAYER:
Let us pray that the love of Christ may liberate us from narrow pre-occupation with ourselves.

READINGS:
1) **Dt. 6:2-6.** Our Jewish brothers still pray a part of this passage from Deuteronomy each day: "Listen, Israel, the Lord our God is the one Lord. . . ." It is a marvelous confession of the God whose love created the world and fashioned a people.
2) **Heb. 7:23-28.** The reading from the Letter to the Hebrews assures Christians that in Jesus we have a priest who will live forever to intercede for us.
3) **Mk. 12:28-34.** In Mark's Gospel, Jesus quotes the passage from Deuteronomy we heard in the first reading. The one law of Christians consists in the indivisible love for God and for neighbor.

HOMILY NOTES:
● In the life of the universe everything happens in its appointed order according to the laws of nature — the movement of the planets, the succession of the seasons. In our Christian life, too,

there is appointed order in the two great laws that are inseparable and that Christ has given us — to love God and to love our neighbor.

● Previous ages may have emphasized the first commandment at the expense of the second. We are perhaps in danger of the opposite emphasis.

● Both commandments must be obeyed. We cannot truly love God if we do not love our fellowmen (1 Jn. 4:20-21). In loving our neighbor we love Christ in him and in that way are led back to the Father.

● Loving our neighbor includes concerning ourselves in questions of world poverty, war and peace, disarmament, and racial justice.

GENERAL INTERCESSIONS:

Invitation: If it were not for Christ, our prayer would have neither value nor meaning. It is only because we share Jesus' priesthood in faith and Baptism that we can stand as brothers before the Father and make intercession for the world. Let us do that now, as we respond: **HEAR US, GOD OUR SAVIOR.**

1. That we may remain faithful to the heritage we share with our Jewish brothers, the heritage that confesses God's unity and love for mankind, we pray to the Lord.

2. That the Holy Spirit, the Comforter, may calm our fears and lead us into a bold, confident love of the Father, we . . .

3. That Jesus' prayer for the unity of those who believe in him may give hope to those working for ecumenism, we . . .

4. That our daily cares and preoccupations may never lead us into forgetting about the millions whose lives are eaten away by disease, we . . .

5. That our share in Christ's priesthood may make us conscious of our responsibility to pray constantly and never lose heart, we . . .

(Additional invocations) _____

Conclusion: Father, your Son gave us a new commandment of love to show that we are his disciples. We confess that there are times when his new law has seemed beyond our powers to fulfill or understand. Help us, today, again to start loving and living like brothers, through the same Christ our Lord.

ADDITIONAL INVITATION TO COMMUNION:
Behold Jesus, always living to intercede for us!

PRAYER AFTER COMMUNION:
"You must love the Lord your God with all your heart, with all your soul, with all your mind and with all your strength . . . you must love your neighbor as yourself." Let us pray for an understanding of what it means to love one another as Christ has loved us.

Thirty-second Sunday of the Year

THEME: THE POOR IN SPIRIT

INTRODUCTION:

If poverty were a matter of sheer economics, one could approach the problem by a sophisticated use of math and sociology. But being poor is more than being out of cash; poverty affects the total person in his outlook on God, on the world, and on man himself. In the Gospel, economic poverty is no particular virtue; but the poverty of spirit which leads one to live purely in faith and hope will bring a man close to the Kingdom of God.

INVITATION TO PENITENTIAL RITE:

In the Gospel Jesus proclaims that the poor in spirit are blessed because the Kingdom of Heaven belongs to them. Let us reflect for a moment on our attitude toward poverty, especially that poverty which breaks our hearts open to the saving grace of Christ.

FORM C: *(Optional invocations)*

Jesus, friend of the poor and of sinners: Lord, have mercy.
Jesus, offering yourself in sacrifice for sin: Christ . . .
Jesus, revealing salvation to all who wait for you: Lord . . .

OPENING PRAYER:

Let us pray for a poverty of spirit expressed without pretense or hypocrisy.

READINGS:

1) **1 Kgs. 17:10-16.** Two of today's readings concern poor widows. The first one is from the First Book of Kings, and the second from the Gospel selection from Mark. In both cases, the widow expresses poverty of spirit through a total dedication to God's mercy and providence.

2) **Heb. 9:24-28.** When Jesus offered himself for sin, he purified our hearts once and for all to serve the living God.

3) **Mk. 12:38-44.** The widow in today's Gospel is the perfect illustration of Jesus' teaching on poverty. She does not give from her surplus goods, but rather she gives everything she possesses.

HOMILY NOTES:

● The widows in the two readings had very little in the way of possessions. Still, they were prepared to give the little they had.

● Since they had nothing to lose, they were not afraid to be themselves. Their actions were not encrusted with hidden motives. Contrast this with the approach of the Pharisees of the reading. Here the things that count are effort, wealth and position.

● Is our own inner and prayer life like that of the widows or of the Pharisees? Does prayer depend on rational application or on repetition of fixed formulas? Do we relax in a glow of self-satisfaction at our gifts to charity? Or do we rely totally on God's capacity rather than our own?

● In prayer, this means quiet, stillness, few words — "Father, I commit myself into your hands"; "I believe, Lord; help my unbelief." Try to reflect today on the inner qualities of the widows we've read about, and compare our approach to God with theirs.

GENERAL INTERCESSIONS:

Invitation: Poverty is a quality of faith which bespeaks the total dependence of man on God. If we believe in the spirit of the Gospel, we are bound to be both poor and prayerful. Let us pray that God will fill our lives with the presence of his Kingdom, as we respond: **HEAR US, FATHER OF THE POOR.**

1. That we may be truly a Church of the poor, dependent upon God's mercy, rather than upon wealth and position, we pray to the Lord.

2. That our prayer may reflect those Gospel qualities of simplicity, confidence, and childlike trust, we . . .

3. That we may always hunger for the bread of the poor: the Word of God which has the power to transform our lives, we . . .

4. That we may be prepared to meet the living Christ in the persons of the poor, the stranger, the widow, and the orphan, we . . .

5. That Christians burdened by sin and guilt may discover the peace and freedom offered in the sacrament of reconciliation, we . . .

(Additional invocations) _____

Conclusion: Hear us, Father, in your tender love for the poor. May we learn to depend on the bread you freely give: the bread of your word, your sacraments, and your living presence among us, through Christ our Lord.

ADDITIONAL INVITATION TO COMMUNION:

Behold Christ, who promised his Kingdom to those who are poor in spirit!

PRAYER AFTER COMMUNION:

Of the widow in today's Gospel Jesus said: ". . .from the little she had, she has put in everything she possessed, all she had to live on." Let us pray that all who are poor in spirit may find refreshment and peace at Christ's table.

Thirty-third Sunday of the Year*

THEME: THE PILGRIM CHURCH

INTRODUCTION:
During the last few weeks of the Church Year, the readings for Mass invite us to reflect on the final goal of human life and history. We hear Jesus making cryptic comments about darkened suns and bloody moons, about the Son of Man coming in power and glory. All of these strange expressions point to a single reality: a future world transformed by the power of Christ's love. As a pilgrim Church, we are moving toward that future; sometimes we progress slowly, but Jesus has given his promise of ultimate success.

INVITATION TO PENITENTIAL RITE:
The sacrifice of Jesus has guaranteed the forgiveness of our sins, but we remain completely free to accept or reject that forgiveness. Let us ask ourselves if we have been cooperating with the grace which has the power to transform and save us.

FORM C: *(Optional invocations)*
You are the world's future, our hope of glory: Lord, have mercy.
You have guaranteed the forgiveness of our sins: Christ . . .
You will come again in power and might: Lord . . .

OPENING PRAYER:
Let us pray that Christ will transform his pilgrim Church by that glory he shares with the Father.

READINGS:
1) **Dn. 12:1-3.** The prophet Daniel speaks of that future time when time and history will give way to eternity, when just men will be raised up to everlasting life.
2) **Heb. 10:11-14, 18.** The Letter to the Hebrews asserts that the sacrifice of Jesus has sanctified men once for all.
3) **Mk. 13:24-32.** Jesus describes the final consummation of history speaking of violent upheavals in nature. The future, radical transformation of all life and time is symbolized by catastrophic changes in the heavens and on earth.

HOMILY NOTES:
● Our progress towards God is laborious, and, since we form the Church, her road, too, is difficult. The parable of the dragnet suggests that perfection will be reached only at the end of time.
● The Church's progress is patterned by Israel's; there are times of peace and happiness, times of trouble and bitterness, yet always

---

*If the Bishops' Campaign for Human Development is observed on this Sunday, for alternate Mass, see p. 154.

a genuine hope, i.e., expectation, of fulfillment. Christ reconciled God and man: "He has offered one single sacrifice for sins."

● Although this reconciliation is perfect and complete in itself, our part is still required; we must become active members of his Body, the Church, and "make up all that has still to be undergone by Christ."

● The "last days" spoken of by Daniel and Christ are, in a sense, always "these days." So long as we are pilgrims we must expect crises, which can be signs of both imperfections and progress. Being a pilgrim demands sensitivity to change, faith, hope, and perseverence.

GENERAL INTERCESSIONS:

Invitation: Despite crises and upheavals, we make our earthly pilgrimage, relying on Jesus' promise to draw all things to himself in love. Let us pray that Christ will unite his Church and his world in the bond of peace, as we respond: **LORD, SHOW US THE PATH OF LIFE.**

1. That the Church may persevere in living by faith and look with confidence towards Christ as the goal of human history, we pray to the Lord.

2. That persons responsible for planning the world's future may put the rights of human conscience above political and religious ideology, we . . .

3. That Christ, who is our Way, our Truth, and our Life, may give us courage to overcome the difficulties we face in living the Gospel message, we . . .

4. That those who are apprehensive about the future may be fortified in faith by Christ's promise to come again in glory, we . . .

5. For the unemployed, the homeless, and those whose hope has been destroyed through injustice, we . . .

(Additional invocations) _____

Conclusion: Father, all creation longs for your glory to be revealed. Comfort us by your presence and help us to persevere in faith and hope until the heavens and the earth are transfigured in love, through Christ our Lord.

ADDITIONAL INVITATION TO COMMUNION:
Behold Christ the Lord, who is to come in great power and glory!

PRAYER AFTER COMMUNION:
We heard these words in today's responsorial psalm: "You will show me the path of life, the fullness of joy in your presence, at your right hand happiness forever." Let us pray that our union through the Bread of Christ may be the sign of that day when Christ will gather his pilgrim Church into his Kingdom.

Thirty-fourth or Last Sunday of the Year — Christ the King*

THEME: CHRIST, THE KING OF GLORY

INTRODUCTION:

For Americans a celebration of Christ as King may be difficult to comprehend, since our government was instituted precisely out of protest against kingship. Today, in John's Gospel, Jesus confesses that he is a king — but his Kingdom is not of the world, nor is it based on political power and coercion. The Lord Christ rules because he sacrificed his life for our peace; he established a reign of "truth and life . . . of holiness and grace . . . of justice, love, and peace" (Preface of Christ the King).

INVITATION TO PENITENTIAL RITE:

My friends, today's celebration reminds us that Christ should dwell in our hearts by faith, and rule them in truth. Let us examine those dark areas of our lives where we have refused to allow the light of Christ to enter in and heal us.

FORM C: *(Optional invocations)*

Faithful witness, First-born of the dead: Lord, have mercy.
King of glory, whom all men long to see: Christ . . .
Lord of the Church, washing us clean in your blood: Lord . . .

OPENING PRAYER:

Let us pray for the faith to see in the humility of Jesus of Nazareth, God's own Son anointed with the Spirit and with power.

READINGS:

1) **Dn. 7:13-14.** The prophet Daniel gazes into a vision of the night and sees the messianic king of glory.

2) **Rv. 1:5-8.** The early Christian community, meditating on Jesus' life, death, and resurrection, saw him as King reigning in the Father's glory. We share that vision as we listen to our second reading from the Book of Revelation.

3) **Jn. 18:33-37.** Jesus, standing on trial before Pilate, claims no earthly kingship. Rather, he proclaims a Kingdom born out of humiliation, suffering, and death.

HOMILY NOTES:

● The first two readings today speak about the glory of Christ in his second coming. The word "glory" is often used in the Old Testament for the light-filled splendor of the presence of God. So, when

---

*If the Bishops' Campaign for Human Development is observed on this Sunday, for alternate Mass, see p. 154.

*If the Bishops' Campaign for Human Development is observed on this Sunday, for alternate Mass, see p. 154.

Christ appears in his glory, we shall recognize him as the One who could say: "Philip, to have seen me, is to have seen the Father."

● This glory was not so obviously manifest during his earthly life; Christ himself explains why to Pilate: "My kingdom is not of this world." His glory is not the ostentatious glory of riches. He himself tells us what is to be the raw material of that glory that we shall share with him at his second coming: "Come, you whom my Father has blessed . . . For I was hungry and you gave me food . . ."

● The recognition of Christ as King brings other consequences. We are not his slaves. He counts us as members of his family, his brothers, his sisters, his friends. Through our share in his life we are members of a royal race. This demands of us a nobility of life and a spirit of service.

GENERAL INTERCESSIONS:
Invitation: We are mistaken if we base our faith in Christ's kingship on external signs of power and success. Christ reigns as Lord only to the degree that we Christians allow him to live and breathe through his Spirit in us. Let us pray that Christ's Kingdom may penetrate more deeply into our lives, as we respond: **HEAR US, KING OF GLORY.**

1. That Christ's Kingdom of grace and holiness may become present among us, healing our sins and divisions, we pray to the Lord.

2. That all who long for a peace and a justice higher than those devised by human wisdom, may find in Christ's kingship a fulfillment of their longing, we . . .

3. That as Christ's body in the world, we may continue his mission of witnessing to the truth, we . . .

4. That persons for whom life has become an intolerable burden may find the peace of Jesus, the Lord who is gentle of heart, we . . .

(Additional invocations) _____

Conclusion: Father, hear the prayer we offer in the name of Jesus, the King of Glory. Raise us up with him, and help us truly become what you have destined us to be: a Kingdom of priests who can serve you and can love a fallen world back to life. We make our prayer through the same Christ our Lord.

ADDITIONAL INVITATION TO COMMUNION:
Behold Christ, First-born of the dead and King of Glory!

PRAYER AFTER COMMUNION:
Jesus replied to Pilate: "Yes, I am a king . . . I came into the world for this: to bear witness to the truth." Having been fed by the word and the Bread of truth, let us pray that Christ may draw all men toward his coming Kingdom of grace and holiness.

December 8: Immaculate Conception

THEME: MARY'S ROLE IN GOD'S PLAN

INTRODUCTION:

We often get the idea that Mary is important only because she gives us a fine example of humility and virtue. But there is a deeper reason for her significance among Christians: the mystery of Mary's life reveals the deepest mystery of our own. As she was filled, from the first moment of her life, with the grace and holiness of Christ, so we who have been reborn in Baptism are filled with the same grace and holiness. For in Mary's Immaculate Conception we do not celebrate a biological wonder, but the full triumph of grace.

INVITATION TO PENITENTIAL RITE:

In the words of Paul, we Christians were "claimed as God's own, chosen from the beginning." Thus we share with Mary the privilege of intimate union with Christ, of cooperation in the Father's plan for salvation. Let us call to mind the moments when we have been stubborn and uncooperative, unwilling to accept the transforming power of grace.

FORM C: *(Optional invocations)*

In you we find all the spiritual blessings of heaven: Lord, have mercy.

In you we were called to be holy and spotless, dead to sin and alive to grace: Christ . . .

In you we were chosen as God's own sons and daughters: Lord . . .

OPENING PRAYER:

Let us pray that as Mary was filled with grace and the Holy Spirit, we, too, may learn to live through love in God's presence.

READINGS:

1) **Gn. 3:9-15, 20.** The tragedy of human weakness and sin is not the only theme of the first chapters of Genesis. There is also the positive theme of God's promise to save men from the effects of evil through the offspring of a woman. The liturgy thus sees Mary as a "new Eve," the mother of all who are reborn in Christ.

2) **Eph. 1:3-6, 11-12.** Our first reading declared God's promise of future salvation; in the mind of Paul, God planned from the very beginning to call all men to holiness in Christ. This is the subject of our second reading, from the Letter to the Ephesians.

3) **Lk. 1:26-38.** Mary is chosen out of all women to bear the world's salvation, and thus to bring to fulfillment the promise and the plan we heard about in our first two readings.

HOMILY NOTES:

● Sin is inherent in our world, its effects are all around us. But we

138

know that God, through Christ, has reversed the insidious process. Though we live in a sinful world, we know that one day the evil will be overcome and a new age will begin.

● Mary, the chosen instrument of God, is the example of one who accepted a role, perhaps strikingly simple — to be a mother — but immensely demanding, costly of everything that would make life satisfying and comfortable.

● Her readiness to comply, her willingness to listen, her heartfelt obedience are attitudes we should try to imitate. Through our imitation of Mary we too become bearers of Christ to those we meet in our everyday lives.

GENERAL INTERCESSIONS:

Invitation: Though we may be painfully aware of our human weakness and limitation, today's feast tells us we can heartily rejoice in the Lord. We can be joyful because in Mary we see grace more powerful than sin, life stronger than death, goodness victorious over evil. Full of hope, let us pray with the words: **WE ARE YOUR SERVANTS, LORD.**

1. That our hearts may listen for God who calls us to do his will by making full use of our human freedom and imagination, we pray to the Lord.

2. That, like Mary, the Church may ponder the mystery of God's life and love revealed in Christ and revealed in the events of our time, we . . .

3. That the power of the Holy Spirit may come upon us, so that his gifts of serenity and peace may be manifest in the world, we . . .

4. That persons in responsible positions of government may learn that wisdom is often to be found in quiet listening rather than in frantic activity, we . . .

5. For all who have committed themselves to a life of celibate chastity for the sake of the Gospel, we . . .

(Additional invocations) _____

Conclusion: Blessed are you, Father, for you choose the weak and humble of this earth to reveal the glory of your grace. We rejoice in the goodness of Mary and ask that we who were reborn in Baptism may be filled with the same grace and holiness that was hers, through Christ our Lord.

ADDITIONAL INVITATION TO COMMUNION:

Behold Christ the Lord, whose holiness flooded Mary's heart from the beginning of her life!

PRAYER AFTER COMMUNION:

"In Christ we were claimed as God's own, chosen from the beginning, under the predetermined plan of the one who guides all things." Let us pray, renewing our faith in God's plan and our dedication to its fulfillment in us.

March 25: The Annunciation

INTRODUCTION:

The early Fathers of the Church once said that Mary conceived Christ in her heart long before she conceived him in her body. Indeed, Mary's attitude of humble obedience to the Word of God is still instructive for Christians. She was not a naive and colorless personality, but rather a woman fully alive and fully responsive to God's creative will. Today's liturgy invites us to open our hearts and our minds obediently to the Word of God, with all its surprises and unexpected implications.

INVITATION TO PENITENTIAL RITE:

My brothers and sisters, we should not confuse obedience to God's will with an attitude of blind slavery. The Lord seeks our cooperation as free human agents with ideas and potentials of our own. Let us ask ourselves if we are growing in free response to God's will, or if we have been content to float along without serious attention to his call.

FORM C: *(Optional invocations)*

The truth of your Word calls us to freedom: Lord, have mercy.
The strength of your life overcomes our fear: Christ . . .
The knowledge of your love leads us to holiness: Lord . . .

OPENING PRAYER:

Let us pray, together with Mary the Mother of Jesus, for hearts ready to obey God's call to greater holiness.

READINGS:

1) **Is. 7:10-14.** Isaiah informs us that Ahaz the king was involved in a common human predicament: he was afraid to let go of his own carefully laid plans in order to allow for a surprising sign from God. But God's sign is given anyhow: a son will be born of a young maiden.

2) **Heb. 10:4-10.** The Letter to the Hebrews explains that, from the moment of his coming into the world, Christ was bent on one thing alone: obedience to God's will for our salvation.

3) **Lk. 1:26-38.** Luke describes the moment when the word of God and the word of a woman meet and embrace. God invites Mary to receive the Word, and she responds with an obedient "Yes."

HOMILY NOTES:

● God asked Mary to accept a particular role and, through her consent to God's word, she became the mother of Jesus. Mary's obedience and faith are the means by which salvation came to the world.

● She responded fully and completely. Mary loved so much that she never faltered in her response to God's invitation. She is our perfect example of acceptance: "Behold, I am the handmaid of the Lord."

● This is a lifelong thing. To give up our own way and respond to what is asked of us is not easy. Turning away from self towards God requires continuous and ever changing response to meet the different demands and circumstances of our lives. We should not simply go around doing our duty or fulfilling obligations, but meet every situation with a free and generous heart asking ourselves how God would have us act.

● "For you were called to freedom, brethren; only do not use your freedom as an opportunity for the flesh, but through love be servants to one another." Blind obedience is not enough — we must respond creatively with heart, mind and will.

GENERAL INTERCESSIONS:

Invitation: Both Jesus and Mary were persons utterly free, yet totally dedicated to the fulfillment of God's will in them. They faced the full consequences of such obedience, even when that meant pain, misunderstanding and finally death. Let us pray for such dedication to God's Word, as we respond: **LORD, YOUR WILL BE DONE.**

1. That we may share Mary's faith in the Word, and follow God's will with joy, we pray to the Lord.

2. That the Holy Spirit may overshadow the Church, filling it with obedience in faith and fruitfulness in good works, we . . .

3. That as Mary's body became the dwelling-place of the Word, we may honor our own bodies as temples of the Holy Spirit, we . . .

4. For all our mothers, living and deceased, that God may bless the sacrifices they have made for us, we . . .

5. For persons who devote their lives to the study and contemplation of God's Word in Scripture, we . . .

(Additional invocations) _____

Conclusion: Father, send the Holy Spirit upon us, so that we may hear your Word in faith and fulfill it in our lives. Give us hearts that are joyful and obedient, ready to do your will in every thought and deed, through Christ our Lord.

ADDITIONAL INVITATION TO COMMUNION:
Behold Christ, ever obedient to the Father's will!

PRAYER AFTER COMMUNION:
" 'I am the handmaid of the Lord,' said Mary, 'let what you have said be done to me.' " Let us pray that we may be ready to obey God's Word even when it seems to demand hard and foolish things of us.

141

June 24: Birth of John the Baptist

THEME: THE MAN WITH A MESSAGE

INTRODUCTION:
John the Baptist was a man burning with a message about repentance and the imminent coming of God's Kingdom. But John's
mission was particularly delicate, even frustrating: he did not live to
see the final fulfillment of the promise he announced. The Church
has a good deal in common with John: it points not to itself, but
solely to Jesus Christ as the presence of God's Kingdom and the
fulfillment of our hope.

INVITATION TO PENITENTIAL RITE:
John's mission was, in the words of the Gospel, "to prepare for the
Lord a people fit for him." That mission continues still, for we are
always in need of conversion and purification. Let us prepare our
hearts for the Eucharist by opening them to the searing power of
God's word, which can burn away our sins.

FORM C: *(Optional invocations)*
You cleanse our hearts by the message of the truth: Lord, have
    mercy.
You fill us with the joy of faith and repentance: Christ . . .
You send us the Holy Spirit as the forgiveness of our sins: Lord . . .

OPENING PRAYER:
Let us pray that our lives may direct the world's attention to Jesus
Christ, God's living Son and brother to every man.

READINGS:
1) **Is. 49:1-6.** Usually the Servant songs of the prophet Isaiah are
applied to the person and mission of Jesus. Today, however, John
the Baptist leaps to our minds as we hear the words: "I will make
you the light of the nations."
2) **Acts 13:22-26.** The missions of John the Baptist and Jesus were
intimately associated. Paul's speech, in our passage from Acts,
reminds us that Jesus' coming was heralded by John when he
preached the baptism of repentance.
3) **Lk. 1:57-66, 80.** John's birth caused a great sensation among the
people; they wondered who the child would turn out to be.

HOMILY NOTES:
● The first reading comes from one of the songs about the Servant
of the Lord. Much of what is said there is true of John the Baptist,
who gave his life to herald the coming of Jesus, and who had to
face the temptation of feeling that his own work had been futile.

- John saw himself as a voice that announces a great event, a finger pointing towards some distant figure, a weapon in someone else's hand. To the people who thought he must be the one from God he said plainly: "I am not he. No, but after me one is coming."
- He was a strange, disquieting figure to his contemporaries. From his birth there had been signs and events to puzzle and awe the onlookers. "What will this boy turn out to be," they asked one another, "a prophet, a leader, a priest?"
- Jesus gave the answer. "John," he said, "was more than a prophet. This is he of whom it is written, 'Behold, I send my messenger before your face who shall prepare the way before you.'"

GENERAL INTERCESSIONS:

Invitation: John appeared to Israel with a message of hope, and he remained faithful to that message even when it seemed futile and unproductive. Let us pray for the courage to preach the Good News of Christ both in season and out of season, as we respond: **LORD, WE LONG FOR YOU.**

1. That the Spirit may set men on fire with a love for Christ and a desire to spread the message of truth, we pray to the Lord.

2. That John's birth as a prophet of repentance may lead Christians to re-examine their lives to see if they are really in accord with the Gospel, we . . .

3. That the Church may prepare the way of the Lord's coming by promoting justice for men who are victimized by crime and violence, we . . .

4. That the bloodshed of war may give way to Christ's way of peace, we . . .

5. That John's coming as a light to the nations may encourage all men who live in the dark shadow of death, we . . .

(Additional invocations) _____

Conclusion: Father, we gather as your Church to celebrate the birth of a man who was fearless in preaching your name and your Kingdom. Help us, a people reborn by water and the Spirit, to witness to your love even to the ends of the earth, through Christ our Lord.

ADDITIONAL INVITATION TO COMMUNION:
Behold Christ, whom John heralded as God's tender mercy among men!

PRAYER AFTER COMMUNION:
The people who heard of John's birth wondered: "What will this child be?" and "Was not the hand of the Lord upon him?" Let us pray that, like John, we may herald the Lord's salvation to all men who live paralyzed by fear and distress.

143

June 29: Peter and Paul

THEME: WORDS FROM PRISON

INTRODUCTION:

Peter and Paul changed the lives of great numbers of people because they brought Christ's teaching to them and made them members of Christ's People. Neither man ever had illusions as to the source of his influence.

INVITATION TO PENITENTIAL RITE:

My friends in Christ, we too are called as apostles to share the Lord's sufferings so as also to share his glory. Let us ask God for courage to move forward out of the prisons of self-interest and into the freedom of his faithful service.

FORM C: *(Optional invocations)*

You lead us into freedom by the victory of your cross: Lord, have
   mercy.
You forgive our sins through the gift of your Spirit: Christ . . .
You give us hope for the future by your promise to come again:
   Lord . . .

OPENING PRAYER:

Invitation: Let us pray for the wisdom to carry on the mission of Christ as true apostles and prophets of his Kingdom.

READINGS:

1) **Acts 12:1-11.** God's will for our freedom and holiness exceeds our wildest dreams. In this passage from Acts, Peter discovers that his deliverance is not a dream but a living reality.

2) **2 Tm. 4:6-8, 17-18.** Apostles may be imprisoned, but God's Word cannot be silenced. Today we hear Paul give thanks for his share in spreading the Good News of Christ.

3) **Mt. 16:13-19.** Who is Christ and what does he mean for us? Peter's answer to this question brought him strength and forgiveness; it can do the same for us.

HOMILY NOTES:

● Of the twelve apostles, it was Peter who first recognized Jesus for who he truly was. "You are the Christ, the Son of the living God." Peter was a happy man, Jesus said, because his insight was due to God's initiative and not his own.

● The first reading shows Peter in prison for the sake of Jesus. The second reading comes also from prison, and this time it is Paul who writes. Both men have behind them years of teaching, travelling, danger, achievements and persecution.

● Peter is amazingly rescued from prison and he attributes it immediately to God; he is certain that God will keep him safe for the work still to be done. Paul does not look for rescue; he knows that his work is done and his life is now at its very end. Looking back on it, he writes: "The Lord stood by me and gave me power so that his whole message might be proclaimed."

● What Paul said, Peter's life declared equally plainly. Both of them realized that whatever they had achieved had been done through God's power, not their own, that everything was due ultimately to God's initiative.

GENERAL INTERCESSIONS:

Invitation: The Vatican II described the Church as a household where the good things of salvation are shared among men. Let us give thanks for our lives together in the Church, as we pray: **LORD, REMEMBER YOUR PEOPLE.**

1. That those who guide God's People as pastors may do so in joyful and responsible service, we pray to the Lord.

2. That those imprisoned by hatred, violence and fear may be freed through the light of the Gospel, we . . .

3. That Christians everywhere realize their vocation as apostles through service to all who are needy, we . . .

4. That all who suffer in mind or body may be healed by the Spirit of Jesus working in our midst, we . . .

5. That we may learn to forgive those who hurt us, and love those who speak out against us, we . . .

(Additional invocations) _____

Conclusion: Father in heaven, every good and perfect gift comes from you. Renew in our hearts the power of your Spirit and give us strength to go on believing in the face of doubt, to go on caring in the face of apathy, to go on loving in the face of opposition. We make our prayer through Christ our Lord.

ADDITIONAL INVITATION TO COMMUNION:

Behold him who gave himself up as a prisoner to make us his brothers in freedom!

PRAYER AFTER COMMUNION:

"You are the Christ, Son of the Living God." Let us pray that the Lord will make us more alive to his presence in the world, and more sensitive to his suffering in the poor and neglected.

August 15: Assumption of the Blessed Virgin Mary

THEME: MARY'S GLORIFICATION, A SIGN OF THE CHURCH

INTRODUCTION:
Every celebration in honor of Mary is, at the same time, a celebration of Christ and of ourselves. For Mary's glorification is a sign of what Jesus' resurrection has gained for all believers. Like each one of us, Mary's share in the glory of Christ is the work of grace: what happened to her is intended to happen for the whole Church. Our feast today is a great sign of hope and of longing for that day when, as Paul says, "all men will be brought to live in Christ."

INVITATION TO PENITENTIAL RITE:
The greatness of Mary lies in her simple openness to God's will: she gave her heart and her body as a dwelling for the Word, and was in turn filled with the risen life of her Son. Let us ask ourselves how responsive we have been to the presence of Christ in our midst.

FORM C: *(Optional invocations)*
Victory and power be yours; for you have crushed death: Lord, have mercy.

Praise and thanksgiving be yours; for you have destroyed sin: Christ . . .

Honor and blessing be yours; for you have brought us all to life: Lord . . .

OPENING PRAYER:
Let us pray that, as Mary shines now with the risen glory of Jesus, so the Church may be brought to that same destiny.

READINGS:
1) **Rv. 11:19; 12:1-6, 10.** The liturgy uses a text from the Book of Revelation to describe how Christ, the son of Mary, has conquered the forces of evil. Our passage also speaks of the Church's battle against destructive powers, with an assurance of final victory through Christ.

2) **1 Cor. 15:20-26.** Paul, writing to the Church at Corinth, explains that, as all are destined to die, so also are all men destined for life in Christ.

3) **Lk. 1:39-56.** From Luke's Gospel we hear Mary's hymn of praise for the great things God will accomplish through her. Because she heard God's Word in joyful faith, all generations of men will call her blessed.

HOMILY NOTES:

- The Assumption was recently defined. How relevant is this feast which we are called to celebrate in honor of Mary?
- The meaning of this mystery celebrated by Christians from very early times is, paradoxically, found in the statement in Paul's epistle on Christ: all men will be brought to life in Christ. For the Father raised Christ from death; so those united to Christ in faith and charity will, by God's power, be given a new life.
- What is this life like? Jesus said it would be abundant and vigorous. By his obedience to his Father's will he vanquished sin, death, the dragon who represents evil. His life was renewed in God. And all who are united to him, will have a life renewed.
- So Mary, the mother of Jesus, by her readiness to love and follow God's will, is, after her Son, the first whose glorification we acclaim. "All generations will call me blessed." God not only blessed her in her privileged motherhood but, because she heard his word and kept it, has made her a resplendent sign to us of the triumph we are promised over evil, in the power of Christ.

GENERAL INTERCESSIONS:

Invitation: Sometimes we are afraid to ask great things of God because we fear disappointment or disillusionment. But today's feast assures us that we are destined for the greatest of gifts: an unending share in Jesus' risen life. Full of this joy and confidence, let us pray: **LORD, SHARE YOUR LIFE WITH US.**

1. That, as all of us have died with Christ in Baptism, we may be raised with him to a full, new life, we pray to the Lord.

2. That, like Mary, the Church may open its heart fully to God's Word and proclaim that Word with joy to all peoples, we . . .

3. That Christians may be known more for honest, humble service than for adherence to power or prestige, we . . .

4. That, in union with Mary the Mother of Jesus, we may be constant in prayer and in seeking to fulfill God's plan for our salvation, we . . .

*(Additional invocations)*_____

Conclusion: Father, we praise your goodness revealed in Mary, the Mother of your Son. As she shares now in his glory, so let us, your Church, grow into that fullness of Christ which you have promised to all who love you, through the same Christ our Lord.

ADDITIONAL INVITATION TO COMMUNION:

Behold the risen Savior, in whom all men are brought to life!

PRAYER AFTER COMMUNION:

Elizabeth spoke to Mary and said: "Of all women you are the most blessed." Let us pray that, as we have been blessed by sharing in Christ's table, we may be brought with Mary to the full glory of his Kingdom.

November 1: All Saints

THEME: HAPPINESS

INTRODUCTION:
Almost everyone agrees that happiness is what men long for, even if they disagree on the means for its achievement. Yet it may come as a shock that the people Jesus described as happy are the very ones we might consider naive or deprived: the gentle, the merciful, the persecuted, and the pure in heart. Have we ever taken these words of Christ seriously? If we did, they would revolutionize our way of life — and make us saints in the process.

INVITATION TO PENITENTIAL RITE:
Because we are frequently confronted with the pain and violence of contemporary society, it is possible that we may assume the role of "prophets of gloom." Perhaps we need to look once again at the example of the saints: they were able to rejoice even in the midst of catastrophe because their hearts were fixed on the joy of Christ. Let us pause to ask God to purify our hearts and to fill them with that peace which the world cannot give.

FORM C: *(Optional invocations)*
We seek your presence, for it alone comforts our sorrow: Lord, have
mercy.
We long for your peace, for it alone brings us joy: Christ . . .
We hope for your coming in glory, for it alone will transform the
world: Lord . . .

OPENING PRAYER:
Let us pray that we who were washed in the blood of Jesus the Lamb may join the saints in singing his praise.

READINGS:
1) **Rv. 7:2-4, 9-14.** Like some of the other New Testament writings, the Book of Revelation was probably written to give support and encouragement to Christians harassed by persecution. John's vision of the 144,000 is a ringing affirmation of God's power to save those who believe and are baptized in the blood of the Lamb.
2) **1 Jn. 3:1-3.** The Christian, as a child of God, must always live by hope. And what he hopes for, St. John tells us, is a future when he will be transformed by the vision of God as he really is.
3) **Mt. 5:1-12.** Jesus promises the happiness of his Kingdom not to the tycoons of powerful influence, but rather to those whom the world regularly ignores: the poor in spirit, the gentle, the peace-makers, and the pure in heart.

HOMILY NOTES:
● The Kingdom of God is not just for the next world. It is for us to

build it up here and now. Jesus tells us the kind of people who belong to the Kingdom: the poor, the gentle, the sorrowful, the single-hearted, those whom our world calls "unlucky."

● But Jesus calls them happy. These are the fortunate people, because nothing stands between them and God. They find their happiness in him because they are not blinded by more transient joys.

● All men are made for happiness, but true happiness is found only in self-forgetfulness, in making other people happy. Following Christ will bring happiness, but it is not easily bought, since it means giving ourselves to others completely as Jesus did.

GENERAL INTERCESSIONS:

Invitation: The happiness for which Christians long is not the mindless pursuit of profit and pleasure, but rather that transforming moment when, as St. John says, we shall see God "as he really is." Let us pray for this happiness, as we respond: **WE LONG TO SEE YOUR GLORY.**

1. That we may offer the constructive criticism of the Gospel to men addicted solely to standards of profit and productivity, we pray to the Lord.

2. That we may serve Christ faithfully, with gentle and peaceful hearts, we . . .

3. That we may promote unity among men by seeking to understand and appreciate the values held dear by people of other faiths and religious traditions, we . . .

4. That the communion of God's saints may encourage us to place the service of Christ above personal desires for attention and acknowledgement, we . . .

5. That the poor may be refreshed by our willingness to give time and love in addition to financial support, we . . .

*(Additional invocations)*_____

Conclusion: Father, you are the unending joy of all the saints: you are the comfort of those who mourn, the peace of those who struggle, and the justice of those who are persecuted. We ask you to unite us all in the communion of those saints, who daily give you praise and thanksgiving through Christ our Lord.

ADDITIONAL INVITATION TO COMMUNION:

Behold Jesus, whose blood gives us entrance into the Father's Kingdom!

PRAYER AFTER COMMUNION:

"Think of the love that the Father has lavished on us, by letting us be called God's children." Having eaten the Bread that makes us one body in Christ, let us pray that he will unite all men in the happiness of that heavenly banquet which promises eternal life.

November 2: All Souls

THEME: PLACE IN GOD'S HOUSE

INTRODUCTION:

It would be ridiculous to deny that death is frightening; its apparent finality wrenches us away from the familiar world of persons and events we have known and loved. Yet death is not all terror and upheaval: it is the final step of that Baptism by which we were united to Christ in his own dying and rising. It is quite true that for Christians death is not something awaited, but something *already done*. What we await is our entry into undying life, that moment when we can say with St. Paul: "Death, where is your victory? Death, where is your sting?"

INVITATION TO PENITENTIAL RITE:

Brothers and sisters, the Christian life is a progressive death to sin, so that the life of Jesus may be manifest in our mortal flesh. We share, with those who have already died, the hope of a glorious resurrection. Let us ask ourselves how often we have consented to the power of death by losing hope in Christ's victory over sin.

FORM C: *(Optional invocations)*

When we were helpless and alone, you died for our sins: Lord, have mercy.

When we were exiled far from the Father's house, your love brought us back: Christ . . .

When we were frightened and miserable, you reconciled us with our God and Father: Lord . . .

OPENING PRAYER:

Let us pray that all who have died in the peace of Christ may be raised up in the body to live with him forever.

READINGS:

1) **Wis. 3:1-6, 9.** The Book of Wisdom, written only half a century before Christ, witnesses to the growing belief in a joyful immortality for those who have put all their trust and love in God.

2) **Rom. 5:5-11.** Because God's love has been poured into our hearts through the Spirit, we can be assured that Jesus has offered his life for our peace and reconciliation. Such is Paul's hopeful message for us in the Letter to the Romans.

3) **Jn. 14:1-6.** Jesus has gone to prepare a place for us in the Father's house. More than that, he has himself become our Way, our Truth, and our Life.

HOMILY NOTES:

● Three somber words stand out in the first reading. They are "death," "disaster," and "annihilation." The writer of the Book of Wisdom sees beyond these and tries to turn the thoughts of his hearers to something more positive.

● He offers, instead, the words, "peace," "hope," and "love." These, he says, are what the dead find in God; these, together with the flowering of all their hopes.

● In the Gospel we hear Jesus himself speaking. He emphasizes that in his Father's house there are many places. There is room for all sorts of people, regardless of how men may judge their worth. Access to these places, to this close relationship with God, is only possible through Jesus. He alone can and does judge the worth of men; and only he knows the hopes and fears and strivings of each one of us.

GENERAL INTERCESSIONS:

Invitation: We pray for the dead not as people without hope, but as a community united with those who have gone before us in the living body of Christ. Let us pray for all the dead, both those known and those unknown to us, as we respond: **LORD, HELP US RETURN TO YOU.**

1. That all who have died in the faith of Christ may dwell forever in the Father's house, we pray to the Lord.

2. That those who have died alone, unwanted and unmourned, may be filled with the light and joy of Christ, we . . .

3. That persons who have died through acts of violence and war may find a place of peace and justice in God's Kingdom, we . . .

4. For the members of our parish who have died recently, and for their families, that they may be comforted by our charity and our prayer for them, we . . .

5. That this Eucharist, which celebrates the dying and rising of Jesus, may be for us the pledge of everlasting life, we . . .

*(Additional invocations)*_____

Conclusion: Father, the power of life and death is in your hand. We pray now especially for those who have died in your peace and for those who have died alone and comfortless. Lead them into your heavenly Kingdom, and unite us all one day in the glory of your presence, through Christ our Lord.

ADDITIONAL INVITATION TO COMMUNION:
Behold Christ, risen in glory to give life to the dead!

PRAYER AFTER COMMUNION:
"I am going to prepare a place for you, and after I have gone . . . I shall return to take you with me." Let us pray, uniting ourselves with our brothers who have died in faith, and ask that we may be with them forever in the Father's house.

Mass for World Day of Peace*

THEME: PEACE AND FORGIVENESS

INTRODUCTION:

According to John's Gospel the first gift of the Risen Lord to his disciples was the gift of peace. For followers of Christ this peace is closely related to the gift of the Spirit and the gift of mutual forgiveness. Indeed, apart from the ability to forgive and to be forgiven, there can be no peace worthy of the name. And what is true of men in their personal relations with one another is true also of nations. No human effort to establish peace on earth will be successful unless it is rooted in a profound respect and charity — the kind of charity which prompted Jesus to lay down his life for his friends.

INVITATION TO PENITENTIAL RITE:

My brothers and sisters, we still need to learn that the meaning of peace can be discovered only if we learn how to make the sacrifice of mutual pardon. Let us seek forgiveness for the times we may have been stubborn, insensitive, and unforgiving.

FORM C: *(Optional invocations)*

Your life is a sign of peace for all men of good will: Lord, have mercy.

Your passion and death is the source of our forgiveness: Christ . . .

Your Holy Spirit is the seal of a new life and a new hope: Lord . . .

OPENING PRAYER:

Let us pray that Jesus' promise of peace may soon find a fulfillment in the lives of all men and all nations.

READINGS:

1) **Is. 9:1-6 (Lectionary No. 831, 1):** Traditionally this passage from Isaiah about the "Prince of Peace" has been applied to the life and mission of Jesus. The prophet seems to look forward to a time when wars will give way to a peace founded upon principles of justice and integrity.

2) **Col. 3:12-15 (Lectionary No. 832, 2):** Paul writes to the Colossians, reminding them that Christ's peace will reign in their hearts, if they learn how to love and forgive one another.

3) **Jn. 20:19-23 (Lectionary No. 835, 4):** The Risen Christ brings his disciples peace through the Holy Spirit and forgiveness.

HOMILY NOTES:

● Human plans for peace certainly deserve our commendation and

---

*NOTE: The Mass for World Day of Peace may be celebrated on January 1 or on another day, according to the judgment of the local Ordinary. The theme above depends on a selection of readings from the "Mass for Peace and Justice" (Lectionary Nos. 831-835) which may be used.

support. But a just peace can never be a mere matter of human ingenuity and clever diplomacy. Peace without charity is sterile and impermanent. Moreover, in the Christian perspective, peace is something more positive than simple absence of conflict.

● The positive content of Christian peace is evidence in *Colossians:* "Bear with one another; forgive one another as soon as a quarrel begins ... Put on love ... Always be thankful." To the peaceful notions of tranquility and order, Christian faith adds a further dimension: forgiving love. This sort of mutual respect and love must begin in our own hearts, homes, and communities before it can affect larger groups of men and nations.

● Thus it does no good to protest violently about the need for peace unless one is willing to love and forgive as Jesus did — totally, without distinctions and reservations. The way to peace is ultimately the way of the cross. Such a way demands sacrifice and perseverance, but it will be crowned by the final victory of Christ's own risen peace.

GENERAL INTERCESSIONS:

Invitation: The God and Father of Jesus Christ is, above all, a God of peace. Let us pray that his peace may guide and govern our lives, as we respond: **LORD, GRANT US PEACE.**

1. That nations may turn their weapons of war and destruction into tools of peace, we pray to the Lord.

2. That, following the example of Jesus, the Prince of Peace, the Church may continue to serve as a mediator between peoples torn apart by hostility and conflict, we ...

3. That governments may use all the means at their disposal to ease the international tensions which lead to war, we ...

4. For the victims of war and military atrocities, especially innocent children, we ...

5. For those who have died in war and for their suffering families, we ...

*(Additional invocations)*_____

Conclusion: Father, we know that every good and perfect gift comes from your love. Grant us the gift of your peace, the wisdom of your Spirit, and the courage to sacrifice our comfort for the sake of justice. Forgive our quarrels and dissensions, and help us to replace them with fraternal love, through Christ our Lord.

ADDITIONAL INVITATION TO COMMUNION:

Behold Christ, whose body and blood are the source of our peace!

PRAYER AFTER COMMUNION:

"Jesus came and stood among them; He said: 'Peace be with you.' " Let us pray that, as we have shared the supper of the Risen Lord, we may also share with each other his gift of forgiveness.

Mass for the Bishops' Campaign For Human Development[*]

THEME: THE QUALITY OF HUMAN LIFE

INTRODUCTION:

In his ministry Jesus frequently spoke in parables about the deep mystery of God's Kingdom. But his concern was not limited to "other-worldly" realities alone; he also showed an enormous interest in the quality of human life in this world. He healed persons broken by evil and disease; he was concerned that they have sufficient food and shelter; he comforted those overwhelmed by disappointment and sorrow. Jesus never lost touch with those ordinary human needs and aspirations which make up the fabric of daily life. As disciples of this same Christ, we cannot afford to ignore the issues of poverty and oppression which threaten to destroy and dehumanize men.

INVITATION TO PENITENTIAL RITE:

St. John once asked: "How can the love of God live in a man who is rich in this world's goods, but closes his heart against a brother in need?" Let us spend a few moments applying this question to our own lives.

FORM C: *(Optional invocations)*

Though you were rich, you became lowly and poor for our sake: Lord, have mercy.
Though you were Lord of glory, you suffered to bring us freedom: Christ . . .
Though you were without sin, you bore the cross for our salvation: Lord . . .

OPENING PRAYER:

Let us pray that our active concern for the quality of human life in this world will always be rooted in the charity of Christ.

READINGS:

1) **Dt. 24:17-22 (Lectionary No. 861,1):** In ancient Israel the rights of underprivileged persons (strangers, orphans, and widows) were protected by law. Our passage from Deuteronomy emphasizes the principle that, out of the fruitful abundance of earth's blessings, provision must always be made for the unfortunate and the oppressed.

---

*NOTE: The texts for the feast of Christ the King may be used for this Mass (when celebrated on that Feast); or the "Mass for Those Suffering from Famine or Hunger" (Lectionary Nos. 861-865) may be used. The theme above depends on the latter choice.

2) **2 Cor. 9:6-15 (Lectionary No. 862,3):** The collection of money and goods for those in need was a hallmark of the early Christian communities. In our second reading Paul appeals to the Corinthians' generosity, asking them to perform the "holy service" of supporting their poorer brethren.

3) **Lk. 16:19-31 (Lectionary No. 865,4):** Luke's story of the rich man and Lazarus contains a stern warning: our failure to assist the starving and the suffering may result in our own condemnation.

HOMILY NOTES:

● Vatican II strongly urged the duty of Christians to provide support — both economic and moral — for the underprivileged: "Some nations with a majority of citizens who are counted as Christians have an abundance of this world's goods, while others are deprived of the necessities of life and are tormented with hunger, disease, and every kind of misery. This situation must not be allowed to continue, to the scandal of humanity." (*The Church in the Modern World*, #88).

● What the Council demanded has long been a part of our Jewish-Christian heritage. The Book of Deuteronomy reminded the Israelites that they too were once outcasts, and that this memory should create in them a sensitivity for people who are deprived of the minimum conditions for a decent human life.

● The early Christians continued in this same tradition of active charity. For them, the support of needy men and women was a "holy service," an act of worship which bound the whole community together in joyful thanksgiving.

● Fidelity to the Gospel, therefore, means more than a "take it or leave it" attitude toward the poor. The story of the rich man and Lazarus suggests that a disdain for the unfortunate is tantamount to hardhearted disbelief. For a Christian to remain inactive and unconcerned in the face of widespread human misery is not only a scandal; it is criminal.

GENERAL INTERCESSIONS:

Invitation: We lend support to impoverished and downtrodden persons not only by generous charity but also by constant prayer. Let us pray that we may cooperate with Christ's work of bringing life abundantly to all men, as we respond: **LORD, HEAR THE PRAYER OF THE POOR.**

1. That nations blessed with an abundance of material goods may share their wealth with those who are miserable and destitute, we pray to the Lord.

2. That with the help of the Holy Spirit, the Church may fulfill its mission to preach good news to the poor, freedom for prisoners, and comfort for those in sorrow, we . . .

3. That we may open our hands and our hearts to the poor and suffering in our own communities, we . . .

4. For those who die daily from starvation because no one is interested in their well-being, we . . .

5. For children, especially orphans, who suffer the cruelty of poverty and injustice, we . . .

*(Additional invocations)*_____

Conclusion: Father, hear the cry of the poor and, in your mercy, grant their needs. Help us to become more generous in service, more loving in charity, and more devoted to the welfare of those who need our help. We make our prayer through Christ our Lord.

ADDITIONAL INVITATION TO COMMUNION:
Behold Christ, who loved the poor and gave his life for the sake of justice!

PRAYER AFTER COMMUNION:
"He was free in almsgiving and gave to the poor; his good deeds will never be forgotten." Having been refreshed by the Bread of Life, let us pray that we may continue Christ's mission of feeding the hungry and improving the quality of human life in our own communities and in the world at large.

LB-3000